Are You Kidding Me

Adrian M. Tisdale

Library of Congress Cataloging-in-Publication Data

ISBN 09711235-4-3

Are You Kidding Me

Copyright © 2015 by Adrian M. Tisdale

Cover Design: Adrian M Tisdale & Destiny Publishings
Editor: Destiny Publishings

Dedication

This book is dedicated to my grandmother, Millie Wylie, My mother, Florence Elizabeth, my aunts Naomi Lyons, Willa Wylie and, all the other mothers in the world raising a girl to a woman really should know this pray.

God grant me the Serenity to accept the things I cannot change,

Courage to change the things I can and the

Wisdom to know the difference.

The Serenity Prayer is the common name for an originally untitled prayer by twentieth century American theologian, Reinhold Niebuhr. [See, e.g., Justin Kaplan, ed., Bartlett's Familiar Quotations 735 (17th ed. 2002) (attributing the prayer to Niebuhr in 1943).

Acknowledgments

For their words of encouragement to finish my book, a special thanks to:

Benita
To my friend, this is a friendship that can stand the test of time. No matter how long or the distance between conversations, it's always like we talked just yesterday. I will always love her!

Camilla
This is the sister that GOD gave me to replace the hollowness in my heart of not having a close relationship with my own sisters. I will always love her!

Charles
Without his unconditional support, Love, faith in the Lord and in me this may not have been a dream come true. This will be a loving relationship that I will cherish forever!

Overview

Author Adrian Tisdale takes you on an adventure to peaks your curiosity....These are truly gripping stories of love, lust, commitment, and betrayal. The gripping stories about the women who are shared with the book give true insight regarding women caught between the men they love verses the love for oneself. Follow the stories of generational rites of passage through raising a woman with the right ingredients. "Are You Kidding Me" gives women a heightened sense of knowing self-worth. There will come a time for every woman's life when she must choose self-first. How far are you willing to go for lust or love? ...What are you willing to give away to get it?

Table of Contents

Why do women cheat? Is it truly the same as men or something else?

Introduction

I've always loved that word "women". Note "wo" is in front of the word "men". You already know the famous words, "Behind every great man is a woman". Well, would it not be very exciting for those words to be changed to say, "Before every great man, is a woman". Women will hold the ship together and give credit to their men for steering the ship.

We want men to steer the ship or pretend that they are steering even if they are not really steering. In my lifetime, I have been blessed to have had so many experiences, both positive and negative. I would like to share those experiences as well as experiences of others who have crossed my path.

In this book you will be exposed to encounters that turned into teachable moments. My heart continues to break because in their heart and souls, my sisters often times have made attempts at the rationalization of love vs. lust. We seem to struggle at getting it right. When we buy in to the cycle of "lust" which is not love, we expose ourselves to mental and/or physical abuse.

We all know women young and old who seem to act less than smart. In some cases, it may be a matter of age and wisdom, but they still have not met their wisdom's peak. I have wondered for some time now, "why" when men give us roses, a box of chocolates, and of course don't forget the, "I miss you note". It seems to pull us right back into the chain of abuse. When in fact, we really needed to get out.

What is this tremendous hold over us that we accept such disrespect and disgust? Think about it, are men the new masters of the plantation in the twentieth century? Are we product of slave mentality and we've yielded to the master's (men) invisible whip?

Men hold the soul tie to our heart and souls? *Genesis 34:2-3, "And when Shechem the son of Hamor the Hivite, prince of the country, saw her, he took her, and <u>lay with her, and defiled her. And his soul cleaved unto Dinah</u> the daughter of Jacob, and he loved the damsel, and spoke kindly unto the damsel."*

"This is why it is so common for a person to still have 'feelings' towards an ex-lover that they have no right to be attracted to in that way. Even 20 years down the road, a person may still think of their first lover... even if he or she is across the country and has their own family, all because of a soul tie!" Source: Soul tie - http://www.ministeringdeliverance.com/soul_ties.php

In God's plan, a newborn's umbilical cord stump typically falls off within about two weeks after birth. That's the true beginning of a child's detachment from their mothers. However, some women appear to have the need to be attached to someone. They can't seem to supply nutrients and oxygen to their body and brain to survive and function separate and apart without that soul tie to their men.

In my research, when I talk to men repeatedly the stock response is always, "Women allow us to cheat, so we cheat! Women allow us to beat them, so we continue to beat them!" What is it in us that won't allow us to walk away? Why can't we detach that tie from these men? When we accept this behavior we are teaching them how to treat us. What is the resolve and why do we make excuses for their?

This book is about women and their relationship with the men in their lives. We will also explore their relationship with their daughters and generational abuse. I want to empower you to find your voice in the world and in some case reestablishing your self-image. What is it about the relationship between little girls and their mothers? Better yet, what has happened to the relationship between little girls and their daddy?

When you finish this book you will indeed have a clear understanding of love vs. lust and men's personality traits. This book will; raise awareness in women, inspire you to achieve outside one's self; and instill loving relationships in the hearts of struggling couples. You will learn that relationships require that both parties put in the work. It may not always be easy but can be very satisfying.

This book will make you cry less, love better, and laugh out loud. It's an inspirational manuscript to help women from all walks of life to survive. It may perhaps give some insight on raising a well-rounded woman with the best ingredients.

Adrian's goal is to inspire, grandmothers, mothers, daughters, and granddaughters all over the world to develop an unbreakable family bond, as well as long lasting connections between mothers and daughters.

I hope to inspire women to journey back to their roots, to develop a sense of self-worth that leads to healthy, loving long term relationships. It is my desire that they know and understand that **Lust** is not **Love**, and begin talking among themselves, and spread the word that "abuse" is never acceptable. Do we have GOD's greatest gift of Wisdom? And why are we still not wise?

What is it about when men give us roses, with a box of chocolates and an I miss you note that seems to pull us right back into an abusive situation when we really need to get out. What is this tremendous hold that men have over women that allow them to be treated with such disrespect and distaste? Yes, women allow this type of behavior; and men have stated it over and over again, women allow us to cheat, so we cheat! Women allow us to beat them, so we continue to beat them! What is it in us as women that will not allow that individual woman to walk away?

So, Sister Girl, let's talk about why do some of us continue to make our men responsible for us and our happiness. Are some women missing the necessary ingredients to become a true mate in the relationship?

Would it not be a prodigious ideas, if we could learn how to:

1. We have to stop being or acting gullible. It's really not a good look.

2. Tell the truth even in the bedrooms, so we can demand truth from our mates.

3. Stop faking during intercourse. Instead, be honest and open to new experiences that are comfortable for you. This way you can both feel free to let go and get real pleasure.

4. Create a sense of intimacy and before play so our mental and physical needs are being met. That may mean you have to create a "show and tell" sessions. We know what we like, in and out of the bedroom.

5. Stop putting the needs of everyone before your own. We have to position ourselves first before we can help others.

6. Understand that true pleasure is between the ears not the legs. You must be front and center in your relationship if you are going to move forward. If you know you cannot at least be truthful with yourself and your mate. You may be

very surprised that you both agree not to continue the relationship and not be lovers, but very close friends.

7.   Stop bragging about your relationship. On lookers perhaps may wish they had a long term relationship on the table, and decide they want yours.

8.   Stop looking at someone else's lawn. Yes, I too, left my husband for two years because I was lonely and my needs were not being met after twenty-five years of marriage. He disappeared from our relationship and I was no longer his priority. So, was it his fault or mine? We came back to each other because I discovered that I loved him. We needed each other because we were more than husband and wife. We were friends.

What I have come to realize is that men are not responsible for their women's happiness. As a woman, I must make myself happy. He must make himself happy. When we come together, we make each other happy. Most people will say, "The same way you can't raise an adult over again".

*C*hapter **1** - **R**aising a **W**oman

When you were a girl and your mother spoke to you, did she tell you to be smart, go to college, get a good education, and become financially independent? Did your mom tell you to find that special man that would love you no matter what and money did not matter? Did she tell you to marry rich and do not settle for anyone that could not buy you riches and gold, or did she tell you as long as you had a man the treatment of this man toward you was secondary?

Why do some girls grow up with a high sense of self-worth and others may not? Are young girls being taught to be subservient? Then when they get older they fear outshining their man and is this wise?

Imagine for one minute we have that magic formula for raising a well- rounded woman. Let's see, plenty of love for the **heart**, water for the **body**, a strong dose of self-image for the **soul**, exercise to keep that hour glass **figure**, milk for strong bones to produce pretty long **hair** and **nails**, shopping for **style**, education for **brains**, scruple for **résistance** and last but not least, **sex appeal** to attract that special someone.

I was raised in Brooklyn New York with a very strong willed mother and a step-father that I loved but did not like very much at all. My mom taught self-worth, education, and independence. I realized when I got older something was missing.

Yes, I had several of those ingredients but lacked love. I could not help but get the sex appeal part down because, wow my mom, was off the chain sexy.

My mom had that type of appeal that drew men. I really don't know if it was because she was extremely intelligent or physically attractive. She would always tell us girls, "You need to get an education because no man really wanted a stupid girl." She would also say, "Never let a man make you his back alley girl." This was the one she would repeat all the time, "Never ever love a man more than yourself."

I cannot ever remember my mom talking directly to me about sex. She would tell us things like, don't let the midnight moon hit your face coming into her house because the only thing that's open after midnight are legs. Come to think of it, I can't ever remember her showing me how to apply makeup on my face. I watched her all the time when she was getting ready to go out, but we never had bonding time.

My mom raised all of us, brothers and sisters to always compete with each other regularly. That's the way my mom liked it, because she felt we would get plenty of practice for the real world. However, my mother did not realize that she destroyed the relationships among the siblings. We were so busy trying to surpass each other we forgot to really love one another.

Although we were not close knit, we always had dinner together. My stepdad was not a hamburger and hotdog kind of guy. As a matter of fact, he called that, junk food. We usually only had hamburgers and hotdogs when we were taken to White Castle for those mini burgers or if we had a backyard cook-out.

My mom was a member of the Eastern Stars and a Daughters of Isles. Our stepfather was a mason. He was also an over the road, sixteen wheel, truck driver, and extremely strict. Growing up, we were not millionaires but we were financially well off.

For a long time I thought my mom was miraculous. Both women and men hung on her every word when she spoke because she was an excellent speaker. Her middle name could have been sexy, and she was beautiful. No doubt, if you looked up the word sexy in the dictionary, you would probably find her picture. So, what happen to this well rounded girl, meaning me, at the early age of eighteen? Well, I think the formula was off, too much of this, and not enough of that.

My mother never could bake a cake the same way twice. My grandmother was the baker. We would often wake up in the morning to bake goods and cinnamon rolls. I really loved my grandma and she really loved us. When grandma got sick, we assumed she had the flu or something. We never knew she had a drinking problem until we were much older. I do know she may have had a blameless motivation, if there is such a thing at all.

Grandma had twelve children and every one of them died except two, my mother and uncle. These kids did not always die at birth, some of them at the age of ten or twelve. I was told that my mother was a Siamese twin, conjoined at the neck. When they were separated the other twin died. I never saw my mother's birth certificate, but she had a scar across her neck.

I don't know if they told me that because my mom suffered extreme spousal abuse at the hands of our biological dad. When beating her, he would pull knives and guns to shock her into submission.

It's bewildering, how my dad got remarried and that woman suffered the same fate as my mom. I remember seeing her one day and she had a black eye. She could not cover the marks with makeup. I have a sister born of that union and it's sad I really never got to know her at all. One of my biggest regrets! Sad, but true unfortunately the common denominator or ingredient in that cake was my dad. So, who was at fault in this situation, both of the women or my dad? Why did they stay? And why did it take my mother four children later to get out of that abusive relationship?

When I was young, my grandma used to tell me lots of stories about family, including my dad, and mom. We would sit on the front, screened in porch of our house. I would laugh and laugh. It was so entertaining. I could not wait for another story.

Grandma protected us with her shield from our step dad, because he believed in beating and was extremely strict. I called it a shield because it was some type of power she had. He would not bother us when my grandma was around. One day I could hear my mom, and grandma in a big argument. My mother sent my grandmother away and we were all sad for a long time. All I could think was that my shield was gone.

I spent a lot of time with grandma and I missed her more than anyone. I was named for her by my mother. When I was little we use to eat white cornstarch from the box on the porch while she was telling me stories. I remember my mother always yelling at my grandma about feeding me the cornstarch. I really loved that white cornstarch all over my face. I guess it was more than that, it was the moments and stories grandma shared.

For some reason, when we were young I felt the drinking and violence in our family legacy did not affect us at all. I was wrong, because when you have substance abuse and violence toward any member of the family it impacts all of the family members. I guess it impacted me in a positive way, because being named after my grandmother, I refused to drink.

It was not the same with other family members and violence followed them in their family lives. I chose not to drink alcohol nor do I use drugs. I do know my parents were extremely strict and my stepfather use to beat my younger brother and older sister a lot. Did my mother move into another abusive relationship and why could she not resist those types of relationships? Again, her fault or his? You decide.

My Siblings were always in trouble for something. One day, my stepdad gave my older sister a black eye. My mother said he did not mean to, but he was upset. I really did not know why at the time. Later, I discovered that my sister, who was sixteen, was allowing her boyfriend to climb in and out of her bedroom window to have sex with her.

Her boyfriend Paul lived next door, she had the front room with the window and he used the balcony over the front porch to climb in and out. That was the first time, I saw any real fist violence in our family by way of our stepdad that did not involve a tap with the belt on your butt, or tree switch spanking.

That was the year, I found out what sex with boys meant, I was fourteen. My older sister was two years older. My parents motto was spare the rod and spoil the child, they used to tell us all the time, to look it up, and it's of course in the bible. The scripture reads, "*He who spareth the rod hateth his son: but he that loveth him correcteth him betimes*" (Proverbs 13:24) and "*Withhold not correction from a child: for if thou strike him with the rod, he shall not die. Thou shalt beat him with the rod, and deliver his soul from hell*" (Proverbs 23:13-14). Apart from the legalities, is spanking a good idea? Does it work?

According to the American Academy of Pediatrics, "*about 90 percent of U.S. parents spank, and about 59 percent of pediatricians in a 1992 survey said they support the practice. According to the academy, effective discipline has three key components: first, a loving, supportive relationship between parent and child; second, use of positive reinforcement when children behave well; and third, use of punishment when children misbehave. Many parents these days are fearful of using spanking as punishment, either because of the law or because they fear it teaches violence to their kids*" [1].

"*I wish that all fathers of households stand forth and practice their role. They will use the rod and not permit their children to go astray. Firmness is needed in your world that is filled with laxity, permissiveness, and degradation.* "*Your children have been misled by many who shall answer to the Father. As teachers they have failed in their role.*

Therefore, as parents you must succeed in yours." - St. Joseph, March 18, 1973 [2]. Spare the Rod, Spoil the Child Calvin College Professor's Research Shows Adults who remember being spanked are well-adjusted... [3] Source [1] [2] [3] - :http://www.tldm.org; Copyright © These Last Days Ministries, Inc. 1996 - 2012 all rights reserved.

After that happened my grandma used to tell me more stories about my mother being abused from our biological father, but I really didn't remember him. My grandma used to say, "There's no shame in being abused, the shame is in the abuser", so remember that when you get older.

Surprisingly, I have three memories of my biological father, one, taking us to White Castle for burgers in New York, two, he came to our school trying to kill us with a gun. They said my mother ran all the way to school with bare feet, gun in hand trying to protect us from my biological father. I remember Father Heart from our school taking all of us down to the principal's office locking us in a room. Finally three, when he died, we had to go empty out his apartment. To my amazement, he was an extreme hoarder in his later years. The apartment was packed from floor to ceiling with boxes, soda bottles, newspapers etc... you name it, and he had it.

I could only remember being raised by my stepfather. I must have been too young to remember when my mother left my biological father. For some odd reason, I never got that many beatings from my stepdad and my mother used to say he spoiled me. Yes, I was spoiled. He used to buy me lots of presents and he'd take me horseback riding. This privilege was not extended to my brothers and sisters. I believe he tried harder with me because he knew I did not care. I also looked like my mom and could have passed for her twin when she was younger. The word was, since I looked so much like her, I got away with murder, so to speak.

Growing up, I did not agree with my parents and I guess too much of this and not enough of that, made me run. I wanted out and married the wrong man too early in life. It's like making a cake; you need portions of flour, eggs, milk, oil, water, etc… So instead of using two cups of flour, you use six and not enough milk or eggs.

How do you think that cake would turn out, and would you really want to eat that cake? It's amazing how some moms can bake a cake that turns out perfect each and every time and others will make mistakes over and over again. It's not that they were intentionally bad moms; they did the best that they could with the knowledge and heart of their soul. Did they learn from their mothers the right ingredients to use in cake baking or never really learned at all? Some women just really never learn how to bake that cake just right. And our children suffer from generation to generation.

It's beyond belief that my stepdad did not raise his own children from another woman. They turned out to be doctors and lawyers and us, not so much. It's really generational and your exposure to life and how the mother's poor choices continue to allow them to make those same mistakes, over and over again. Apparently, in future off springs (boys or girls).

Some mothers don't know if they want a chocolate cake, cheese cake, or strawberry short cake. They really believe no matter what type of cake they are making, they can use the same ingredients. Wrong, if you make a chocolate cake you need chocolate and if you want to make a strawberry short cake, you must use strawberries. Yes, the base of the cake ingredients maybe the same, but just like with each child, each cake is unique. So when you are trying to make strawberry short cake and you use black berries, you missed the mark.

I may have grown up with negative experiences but with lots of benefits; I went to catholic school, lived in a very nice home, my parents had money when it counted the most because I remember we had a live in maid for about five to six years of our life. We were the first kids on the block with a very large, huge color television. All the other kids from our neighborhood would come to our house to watch TV.

We owned several neighborhood restaurants. By no means were we poor. However, we were not rich either. I can tell you somewhere along the way, I was missing some type of ingredients. Because, after all of those stories told to me by my grandma, I still could not read the signs of what type of man not to marry.

I married the worst type of "Abusive Man" when I was eighteen years old. I became an abused and battered wife, same as my mother and grandmother before her. I had to find the strength from what I was taught as a young girl to find myself worth and walk away, nine months after I was married. Sad, as strong as I thought I was it still took me nine months. It was disbelief and I did not realize what was happening until it was too late.

One ingredient I would say I was missing was abundant of love to tell the difference between a loving and an abusive non-loving man. I don't believe my mother or grandmother could teach me those things because they were abused themselves. I could not believe it; I was young, never saw the signs or ignored the signs. I wanted out of my parent's house because I was in love with this young man. From that day forward, I really understood what one's self-worth meant and how it **gave** us strength and power.

It's perplexing how the abusive spirit starts. Maybe with a few degrading words in an argument. Then, as the days and months pass, the arguments get louder and louder. Somehow you see this local motive train coming your way and you're just sitting on the train tracks, thinking it will stop by some miracle.

Finally, it's the day, "the train is here" he punches you and now you are sitting on the floor, crying, with a black eye, maybe a few black and blue bruises. Then wait, wait on it, here it comes he said it *"you made me do it"*. You believe it, so now he is chipping away at your self-worth.

Then of course, he brings you flowers, candy and/or you have the best possible love making session in your entire life and it's really intense. You want him to love you to make everything better and of course you think he's really sorry and he loves you, until next time. Why do you think he's really sorry, because the love making is really intense or he's crying all over you with tears? He must be sorry because men don't cry unless they really love you?

Wrong! Again, you believe him. The love making was off the chain and better than you ever remember. His rolling pin is really working its magic. Why wouldn't the love making be off the chain? After all, you just gave him your self-worth, your power, strength and now you are tied even more to his soul. With every stroke, in that love making session, he draining your power, like Kryptonite drained superman

Are you kidding me? You just gave him more of your self-image and your power. Each and every time this happens, he gains more power and your self-image takes a hit. The power gave him, a high, and a "rush" beyond comprehension. Just like a junkie, who takes that first hit of crack cocaine and gets that ultimate high, now they chase that unquenchable high, that unquenchable rush!

Oh, I know, you just thought he was beating up that body, your flesh and not stealing your power. You did not know he was getting an "endorphin rush, a high. Now he has a taste and he loves that feeling of that "endorphin rush", with the intense love making after degrading you or kicking your Bundt cake. **Are you kidding me**…? He's never walking away!

The pattern starts to develop and this has become your way of life, because like a junkie, he can't stop. Like a junkie, he can't give back the self-worth he took from you. He cannot reach that rush, that high. Some woman can dig deep within, find their self-worth, and walk away, while others cannot.

There was a young lady whose husband used to beat her on a regular basis. She protested that he was not an abusive person until he got drunk. I knew she was driving toward traffic down a one way street, toward those very same train tracks I sat on, waiting.

I wanted to run after her and say, "Stop you are going the wrong way. The train is coming. " I wanted to jump into that car, turn it around, and drag her out of the driver's seat because I'd been down that same road. No matter how much I wanted to stop that traffic accident, stop that train, neither I nor any of our friends could get her out of that car, driving toward that train, "that man"!

One day after years of seeing her get abused, he had beaten her out of her clothes. She ran out of the house for her dear life and to my front door, "butt naked". I opened the door. My husband ran and got a sheet to put over her. She continue to cry saying, "Someday it will stop".

I encouraged her to please, pleaseeeeeee....... open her mind to the possibilities that maybe her husband got drunk, so he could beat her Bundt cake?" After all, who was forcing him to continue the alcoholic behavior which causes him to be aggressive? It was like a light bulb went off in her head or the elevator finally reached the top floor.

Not too much time passed after that last beating that she finally left this abusive man. It just never occurred in her that he was getting drunk, simply to use the drinking as an excuse when he beat her up. Getting drunk was his "get out of jail" free card to beat her Bundt cake. I know it may seem like it was something she should have known, but if you're in that situation it's really hard to see another point of view with the same eyes.

Women with a low self-image may not be able to triumph over this relationship and will be swallowed whole without the assistance of others. I know without my strength, my grandmother's and mother's experiences in life, I could have never walked away from my abusive relationship.

I was so ashamed, a woman of my intelligence and the family I came from to get myself in the same situation. That light bulb went off in my head and I remembered what my grandmother told me, "The shame is not in the abused, but in the abuser."

I remember watching a movie with Tom Cruise and Cameron Diaz called, *"Knight and Day"*. While they were on the plane, Cameron Diaz was talking about getting into her car, riding off into the sunset *"someday"*. Tom Cruise said to Cameron Diaz, *"Someday is a code word for never."*

This is what happens when women are in an abusive relationship, they say someday they're going to leave or it's going to stop, which is another term for *"never"*.

What ingredients do you think you're lacking when you were being molded into this woman from a young girl? Sometimes the rearing of a child may have a little twist because the off spring may learn from watching their mother's mistakes, make changes, or adjustments while, the negative lessons or lack of self-worth are imbedded for a long time to come.

Like magic, it continues to pass from generation to generation.

Some young girls grow up with mothers who are, let's say, less than perfect and this young girl will continue to claim, that they themselves will never be like their mother. Yet, years passed, time goes by, and the memory has faded. The woman finds that not only is she making the same mistakes her mother made, she has turned into her mother.

The very last violence I experienced in my life was when I was date raped. At first, I was not going to include this in my book but women need to understand and make every effort to prevent those situations. I am not saying that if you get date raped it's your fault, but here are some pointers to prevent this experience. However, we must take responsibility for our own actions as well.

I was young, I survived an abusive situation with my husband and a year later I started dating. When you're on dates and you are not in for having sex with this man, don't go back to his place. Let him take you home and say your goodbyes at the door in public view. Do not invite him in for a drink, cup of coffee or a late night snack, or you may be that snack.

In my situation, I was at his place and we started kissing on his sofa and I tried to stop, so he stopped. Then he started kissing me again. When I tried to push him away again and leave, then the violence started and he forced himself and raped me. Thirty-six years ago, after being raped women did not run to the hospital or report it to the police. The elder women in my family wanted to get me past it, so it was never mention again.

I was depressed for a long time and did not trust men. One day my grandma told me I should go out and get some sun. I really did not want to leave the house. Once again, my grandma said to me, "Come here sweetie." She held me in her arms and she said I want to tell you something, we were on the front porch. I remembered that front porch from all the stories she told me and the cornstarch I use to eat when I was younger.

She finally said, "Baby, you must get past this, you cannot let a man steal your power, yourself worth." She told me in a sense that the man took a little bit of flesh, but you must rebuild that part of your soul. I cried, we laughed and she told me, "Remember those nice hot baths, we gave you when you were young. Well, it made your "pus..." short for vagina snap right back to its original size." My grandma frankness continued as she shared that my flesh was fine but I had to get my soul whole again and the family would be there to help me.

FAMILY CIRCLE- *"The strength for souls will be found in the family circle"* (Lady, 1972).

She also told me I would be okay as long as I could take back my soul and power. Guess what? My grandma was right. I was more than okay.

I really loved my grandma and for some reason did not have that type of relationship with my mother. We were not sent to counseling at all. The elders in our families spoke to us.

15

That was your counseling. Young ladies, consider seeking out the elder women in your family. Listen to the stories and past those stories on to your children. I would give anything to have my grandma back in this world, she was very special.

These are the things that are important and I will never get a second turn to experience. My great grandmother, grandmother, mother and older sister are deceased. I would cut off my right arm to get anyone of them back. I am the oldest living relative in my immediate family at the young age of fifty-nine, wishing an elder matriarch was still here. It's lonesome without a mother's love. I never knew my great grandmother, my grandmother died in her early sixties, as well as my mom. My sister died at the age of fifty-two. We were all shocked and one year later my only uncle died, my mother's brother.

So, I say to all, your mother may not be perfect because she can't seem to make a perfect cake, but love them just the same. For some reason, we thought our parents were dreadful and wanted to get away from them because they were too strict. Today we have babies raising babies without the self-image and self-worth passed on from our elders and that's unfortunate. I may be missing a few ingredients, but I'm okay. I love myself and know myself worth.

If you do not know or understand the definition of a battered woman then you should read the next few words very carefully. In Johnson v State, Justice Hunstein of the Supreme Court of Georgia adopted these words:

"[B]attered woman (is) one who is repeatedly subjected to any forceful physical or psychological behavior by a man in order to coerce her to do something he wants her to do without concern for her rights".

Battered women include wives or women in any form of intimate relationships with men. Furthermore, in order to be classified as a battered woman, the couple must go through the battering cycle at least twice. Any woman may find herself in an abusive relationship with a man once. If it occurs a second time, and she remains in the situation, she is defined as a battered woman."

If you are in an abusive situation please get help and always remember to repeat these words over and over again, Psalms 23:4 reads as follows, *"For though I should walk in the midst of the shadow of death, I will fear no evils, for thou art with me. Thy rod and thy staff, they have comforted me."*

*C*hapter **2**: **G**eneration to **G**eneration

The Life Cycle

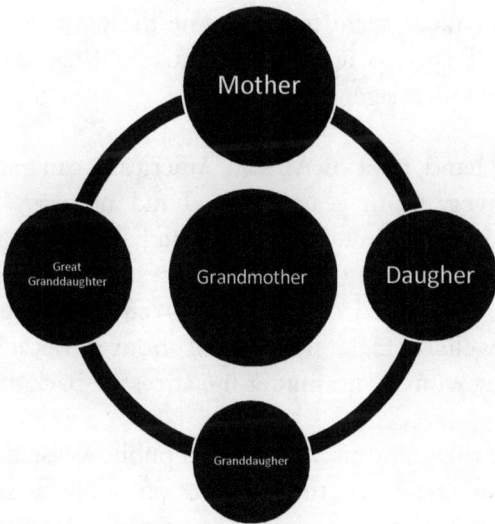

The grandmother gives birth to the mother, the mother gives birth to the daughter, and the daughter gives birth to the granddaughter. All of a sudden the mother becomes the grandmother, and the daughter has now become the mother, and the granddaughter gives birth to her child (great granddaughter) making her a mother and her mother a grandmother. This cycle of life continues to repeat its self over and over again. We must pass on strong values to our children.

I can only write this book as an African American woman. It is my ethnic background that has influenced and shaped my point of view. I have always found that it's amazing how so many other races seem to overcome the darkness of the past. Their off springs appear too prosper financially and have a healthy self-image.

On the other hand, a lot of African Americans can't seem to overcome slavery from years past. I did not say "forget slavery". I said overcome it, two distinctly different things. This is why I say to you the years of ancestral harm, imbedded mistakes are passed on over and over again. Just like generational welfare, make no mistake about it, because this can impact any woman, no matter the ancestral background.

You will have the grandma who was on public assistance, the mom on public assistance, the daughter on public assistance, and the granddaughter on public assistance. It continues because nothing more is being taught about striving for independence, high self-image, and financial wealth from generation to generation. Some women have no aspect of fiscal accountability and it continues through generations.

Are you kidding me? Do you have the right stuff? Did your mom give you all the right ingredients in the right measurements? Are you like the rest of us, lacking something? Whatever those ingredients, today they define you as a woman the woman you are. Are you really in the right spot or is there room for improvement? Do you have time to redefine yourself or do you think it's too late?

Come on. I know what you are thinking, "She does not know me at all. I am, the total package." Really! Do you have your own? Can you support yourself without him emotionally and financially? Can you be by yourself? Can you be happy without him or are you looking for him to make you happy? Have you become one with him and his identity is the only one that will survive? Is it really a fifty-fifty relationship or is it more like ninety-ten? You of course are the giver of ninety percent and only receiving ten? Are you tied to his soul? Should you be?

There are women who are financially wealthy beyond their dreams. Yet, they cannot seem to separate themselves from their man's identity or, "want to be man," in their minds. They continue to put up with infidelity and abuse and do not have the self-image to walk away even though they are financially secure. They have no sense of reasoning and accountability for themselves. On the other hand men will reason their way out of anything. They also inherently use reasoning to get women to do anything they want.

Reasoning is defined: *to think or argue logically, way of thinking, analysis, logic, calculation, reckoning, interpretation, sound judgment and the cause for a belief. How many times have you been arguing or reasoning with and the man comes out on top resulting from this process.*

What is raising a well-rounded woman about? I remember when I was young. I had the influence of my aunt, which made a serious impact on my value system in my latter years. My aunt gave us a sense of reasoning that should have allowed us to make our own choices about what would happen to us. When I was sixteen we were getting ready to go out to a party. My Aunt Naomi sat us down asserting that she wanted to tell us a story about sweet potato pie. At first I said to myself, "what sweet potato pie? We are getting ready to go to a party and she wants to talk about, sweet potato pie." **Are you kidding me…..?**

Aunt Naomi first complemented, by referring to us as very pretty sweet potato pies in our nice new outfits. She hoped we enjoy, and have a wonderful time at the party. Then Auntie educated us. She wanted us to keep an extra token in our shoe, just in case we needed to get home in a hurry, or needed train fare. She said one last thing that stuck with me even until this day.

"I want all of my sweet potato pies to come back whole."

Now you would think being sixteen years old, I would have recognized right away what she was talking about, but I did not. She continued to say again, "I have four sweet potatoes pies and I don't want any slices missing from those pies when all of you come back home. After all, you don't just hand your goodies out to boys; they have to wait to taste those sweets and boys love sweet potato pies." We all laughed. Auntie firmly reiterated, "I mean it, whole pies, no missing slices."

So, in retrospect when I grew up we never really had the "sex talk". It was always express through metaphoric, symbolic stories using goodies, pies, cakes, cookies, and sweets. That night we had a great time at the party and we all listened to my aunt and came home as we had left, whole sweet potato pies. It's remarkable how that story impacted me so much that I remembered it at the age of fifty-nine. I'm sure you have and will note my parallelization of food to intimate situations and body parts.

Incredibly sometimes it takes more than a mom to raise a woman. You want other strong women and elders in the family who set high standards and good examples of moral values. Sometimes, it may take women in the neighborhood. They always say, *"It takes a village to raise a child."* Would our ancestors be proud of us as women? Was the right stuff really passed on to us growing up as young girls to become women? Are we as strong as our women ancestors when they were slaves or are we weaker? After all, they were slaves, and forced to be with men sexually to produce other strong bucks. They were forced to have sex with the master of the plantation not of their own free will, but they were strong women.

We have free will and for some reason, women act in a sense, powerless. Why? Are we as women, enslaved to our men in the worst ways possible? Are the men of today in the year of 2015 the new masters of the plantation, forcing women into compromising positions, taking away their free will to say "no"? Is this the new form of slavery being passed down from generation to generation among young girls? Do we no longer have a strong will, power of choice; to know our worth in this world?

Do they think we are not marvelous the way we are? As a woman, were you taught as a young girl any self-worth, that you are special and have a great deal to offer the world without being abused, and that your man should cherish you for all time? Life isn't about just finding one's self, life is about always continuing to create one's self."

Each time a woman doubts self and/or allows someone else to influence doubts in her mind, you lose a sense of who you are, therefore losing one's self worth. Please always remember, if you think that you are worthy "you are". We as women need to remember our elder women in our family and look back to them to pull our strength to get out of awful situations. Our elders may have been in situations but they pulled themselves out.

We need to remember that we have strong stock in those soup recipes that have kept our families growing from generation to generation. It is only now that we are adding watery issues to the soup which is diluting the stock. Water may be the true essence of life but you can rest assure that you must not add water to everything. Our elders had recipes for soup stock that our children's children don't know. Why are we letting these strong values that we knew as children become lost and not passed on to our children?

When I was raising my son, as boys will do, he would get into trouble at school. I used to say to him, "did you fall and bump your head?"" The reason behind those words was simple. My son was being exposed to other children, and outside elements. The strong influences of other children who spoke back to their parents. Of course this was a period starting a new era of school officials and social workers telling parents that they could not beat their children.

All of a sudden my son felt empowered, thinking he could talk back to me in my own house with no consequence. As a strong mother with values I learned from my mother and grandmother, I stood my ground. I asked him again that day, "Did you fall and bump your head?" Clearly, he must have, to be talking back to me. I sent him to his room with no television that night without spanking. The very next day my son did something in school, he started talking back to his teacher. My son was being disruptive to the entire class? **Are you kidding me?**

My husband had made me a wood butt paddle with holes. When you take that swing, it sucks the butt. One really only needed a couple of good swings with the paddle to make contact to influence correction. He should have gotten that butt whipped that night.

My husband was my children's step-father. As you will recall I was raised by my stepdad as well. Since the passing of generation to generation abuse is learned. I not wanting to risk any possible abuse towards my boys, did not allow my husband to discipline with spankings. However, I wanted my boys to respect my husband. I did the spanking or discipline in the family with our boys. It may have been wrong, but I felt strongly about it because of my past family experiences with my stepdad.

The day after my son disrespected his teacher, I took my wood paddle with the butt holes to school and beat my son in front of his classmates. The next day a social worker came to my house to discuss my method of corporal pun-ishment. She inspected our house and noted on her report that he had his own room, television set, bedroom set, games, and nice posters on the wall. She commented that he had a lot of things and we had a very nice house.

She could not find anything wrong in our home. Now she wanted him to tell her if he felt he was being abuse. That was funny, like he had some type of vote in the family concerning discipline. While she was talking, I heard her telling my son to call her or dial nine 911 if he felt I was abusing him. **Are you kidding me?** Get this, she gave him a business card. This prompted my son to gather this big smile of arrogance. I'm sure he thought he could do what he wanted and mommy would be in trouble if I tried to stop him.

I asked the social worker to please wait a minute. I had some packing to do and it would only take a moment. Then I reiterated for her to please not leave. I went to my son's room and got a suit case and started packing his clothes. My son followed me. He started crying once he realized what I was doing. His crying caused the social worker to inquire as to what was going on. I informed her that my son would be leaving with her, that day.

My son who was in 6th grade of course stood there crying the whole time, saying, "Mommy I don't want to leave home." First, of all she was shocked how this so called little black boy that was supposed to be abused was clinging to me around my body for dear life.

She told me she was not there to take my son away but maybe I needed to go to some parenting classes to avoid any violence in raising my children. **Are you kidding me?** I told the social worker that I would not be taking parenting classes at all. If she or the Commonwealth of Virginia could raise a young black male better than I could in this day and time she was welcomed to attempt. I made it a point to state the following:

1. I was not going to allow disrespect in my household, nor the school from either of my boys.

2. My boys must go to school to learn to read and write (something taken away from us as slaves) and not to act out or talk back to the teachers.

3. My boys would do what I say do, because I brought them into this world.

4. When my son gets out of control because you will not allow me to discipline, then what. I know a great solution, lock my son up with all the other little black boys in jail because they did not have a strong hand in life.

5. I will not be afraid of my children and if they called 911 or her phone number for getting disciplined then be prepared to take me to jail upon her arrival.

6. I love my boys and I was not abusing them. However, they must be respectful in life.

7. I was fighting for my boys lives to keep them from the streets, gangs, and thugs who would only take my boys down a path of no return. Before I would let that happen, they would be gone from my home.

I must say that white woman stood there for about five minutes before she spoke again. When she did speak up, she explained that she was not trying to take my child. Then she started begging me to tell my son he could stay. Also, that I was not sending him away, hoping it will make him calm down. She let me know that she just needed to make sure he was not being abused. I put her concerns to ease by letting her know I understood her position. However, they needed to be careful about the message they were sending our children.

Make no mistake about it, you can turn an otherwise good child into a bad one by making them believe that their parents have no power to discipline them, and there was no consequence for negative behavior or actions. She finally admitted that she could see by my home as well as the way he was reacting, I was not abusing my child.

I countered by letting her know that I do not abuse my boys nor, do I spank them with the wood paddle unless it was necessary. I farther shared that the youngest one had never gotten any beatings with the paddle, but the oldest boy needs it about every four to six months. He was stubborn like his mother and he could really show out at times. I also told her normally, they get sent to their room or they can't go out to ride their bikes, but some instances call for the butt paddle. The same way it called for belts or tree switch spanking from our parents.

Before leaving the social worker assured me that they were closing the case. I never heard from the Department of Social Services again regarding me abusing my boys. And, my son never acted out in school again.

Case Study #2 ~ **Angie's story:**

Several years had passed and I started operating my own business. There was a young lady, who was a single mother that worked for me as a secretary. One day she came to work in tears. She started to explain how she did not know what else she could do with her son who was eight years old.

She let me know that he was out of control. Apparently, the negative behavior began one day after whipping him he called 911 on her. The police were sent to her house. They took a report and referred the case to social services because she spanked him with a switch from a tree.

A lot of African American families used tree switches which are what our parents used to whip us with. They would send you out to the back yard and make you bring them a small thin branch of tree. Sometimes they would soak it in water or you would get spanked when you were coming out of the bath, because it hurt more.

Did our parents get locked up or did they call it child abuse? "No", but that was over fifty years ago. If you were thinking about doing anything bad, you would think twice after you got a spanking with a tree switch. They told Angie she could not beat him and if she did they would put her in jail. The social worker gave her son a business card to report her if she did. Again….**Are you kidding me?** Angie could not believe they gave her son a business card, and he was holding it over her head.

Angie was crying hard. She did not understand why I was laughing. I was reminiscing about when they tried to do the same thing to me several years back when I disciplined my son. She notified me that after they gave her son the business card to report her, his behavior continued to grow worst. He was so out of control that even the schools could not handle his behavior any longer.

The situation left Angie uncomfortable about using corporal punishment on her son. She feared going to jail so she never spanked him again. She shared that the social worker had her son put on Ritalin. **Are you kidding me?**

Ritalin is a medication that is commonly prescribed to treat attention deficit hyperactivity disorder (ADHD), and narcolepsy. Although it is a stimulant that can help people with narcolepsy stay awake and alert, it can also affect certain chemicals in the brain to produce a calming effect in children with ADHD. Abdominal pain, weight loss, and dizziness are some of the common side effects seen with this medication.

So is the message that we can't beat our children for discipline? Nonetheless, we can feed them drugs to control their behavior. **Are you kidding me?** According to Angie, before this situation her son had not been diagnosed with ADHD. I was interested in meeting the young man so I encouraged Angie to bring him to work the next day.

The next day, Angie did as I asked and brought her son to work. I took them both back to my office and they sat in the chairs in front of my desk. I sat in my big chair behind the desk. I wonder if he thought it was a big chair. He was eight years old at that time. I asked him why he was acting out in school and at home. He told me because he could, and no one was going to do anything about it. **Are you kidding me**…? 8 years old!

I said to his mother, "so, he's got a little smart mouth on him." I asked him why he thought no one was going to do anything about it. Do you know that young man pulled out the social workers business card from his pocket? He informed us that she would lock anybody up that beat him. This boy was carrying around that dirty little business card everywhere, each and every day. **Are you kidding me?**

I said, "Really". You think your mom or teachers have no power to control your bad behavior?" He said, "No, I can do whatever I want and nobody will stop me." I told his mother to talk to his doctor and advised him of what was really going on with his behavior. She needed to enlighten them on what happened with the police and social worker. In the meanwhile, I would stop the Ritalin immediately he did not need it; he was just out of control.

I leaned forward over my desk and pointed my finger toward him and said, "Come here". He did not want to nonetheless he leaned forward in his chair. I told him, "This out of control, disrespectful behavior was going to stop, today. Do you understand me?"

He said in a low tone, "Yes". I continued telling him that if he called the police or the social worker on his mother again, I was going to break all those little fingers, so he would not be able to dial any type of phone ever again. He looked at me and grabbed his fingers at the same time. His eyes widened. I raised my tone just a little and said to him "do you understand me young man?" He said, "Yes ma…."

His mom looked at me and looked at him and appeared to be shocked that he had not been so respectful in over six months. I told him that his mother loved him a great deal. Then I asked him, "Do you believe that?" He said, "Yes ma…?" Then I enquired, "Does your mom really abuse you at home?" He answered, "No, ma…," and further explained that he got mad at her for beating him that time and wanted to get her in trouble.

I asked him who told him to get his mom in trouble. He informed me that other kids in school told him to dial 911 to report his mom. This way he could do whatever he wanted without getting a beating. I said, "Okay, but now we understand each other, and that's wrong." He said, "Yes ma." I invited him to come around the desk. He appeared to be afraid but he came anyway. I gave him a great big hug and kissed his cheek and let him know his mom loved him and always would.

I reminded him that his mom would spank him if he got out of control because she loves him. Then I asked if he understood, he said, "Yes ma." I gave him a dollar and told him to have his mom buy him some ice cream. He walked around back to his mom, with tears in his eyes. He gave her a hug and took her hand. I could see tears in Angie's eyes too. They walked out hand-in-hand. Then she dropped him off at school.

Angie also talked to the doctor and they agreed to stop the Ritalin. I encouraged Angie to take her son to an independent counselor so they could question him separate from social services and her influence. She did and guess what? They discovered the same thing I already knew, his mom was not abusing him at all. He simply wanted his way without any consequences to his actions. They closed the child abuse case against her. After three months passed, he was doing much better.

Angie said it was like having her old son back at home, no more outburst and unruly behavior that was uncontrollable. He and his mom showed up with flowers to say thanks. As far as I knew while she was working for me, she never had any more problems from that situation. She brought her son, by the office from time to time. I kind of winked at him and smiled. It was funny. He would laugh and always grab his fingers.

I understand that social workers must do a job to prevent abuse among children, who are really being abused. But there is a fine line and they need to make sure they are not pushing good kids to the dark side, simply to get out of being disciplined. In this situation it took more than this mother to get her child back on track. It took another mother, "me" to get through to this child.

Yes, sometimes it takes a village to raise a child. It's a clear cycle of life and a need to control our offspring, so they can grow up to be healthy and happy in life. Society has a code of behavior and we as great grandmothers, grandmothers, and mothers must teach our offspring from generation to generation what that code of behavior is to survive.

*C*hapter **3**— *A* Sense of Entitlement

"Humanism in your world has been created by Satan. You will bring back the adages of old of: Spare the rod and you will spoil the child. Discipline must be returned to the homes." - *St. Joachim, July 25, 1973*

Source: American Heritage Dictionary: hu·man·ism- A system of thought that rejects religious beliefs and centers on humans and their values, capacities, and worth.

Sister Girls "can we talk"? We as women maybe destroying our offspring? I know we want to raise our children with the best intentions. Of course, what we did not have when we grew up fiscally, we wanted to make it possible for our children. Some of the children of the now generation have no moral fiber, or self-worth. It's almost like having less financial means with more love, gave some of us reasoning and accountability, along with a positive self-image needed to make our own choices Also to be successful in life. Yes, during that period, we still had problems, then again unlike today.

Parents back then did not have the money to simply give us stuff, they spent their time, took us to the park, skating and hosted family activities. Families back then had a weekly tradition of Sunday dinners, holidays, vacations that all of the family attended. It was a bonding time among family members that does not transpire today.

The love of yester-year did not have to always come from our mothers. It may have come from other mothers, but it was love. So did we not really learn the right stuff to pass on to our offspring's?   Have we forgotten Toby from roots, in Alex Haley's book? Toby, was his slave name given to him by his master. He came from Africa but continued to instill a family history into his offspring. He always remembers where he came from with a sense of pride that continued to be passed on to the women and men in their family.

Are we so disappointed with our parents for not having fiscal wealth that we felt we should cut out a sense of accountability, and not pass it to our children? When we grew up my parents had money, but we had popcorn, fruit, food, cakes, and pies with limited toys for Christmas, with a very large family gatherings.

Are you kidding me, there were no personal computers, iPads, iPods, or cell phones to distract family members from spending time together. Is it that, we don't want our children to suffer? Do we want them to have more and not work as hard for it? Are we sending our children the right message? Are we really being smart? Did our parents raise us in a way that is superior to our style of rearing?

Are parents today not the same as our parents who prepared us for "Life" as we know it today. Is it our fault or theirs? Are we giving our children the right ingredients to become young, responsible, reasoning adults who are accountable? It's astonishing how I have watched families over the years, including my own grow. You want to say, "**Are you kidding me**…? Helloooo… Wake up, wake up.

Let's have a rebirth. Let's start over again."

STRONG DISCIPLINE AND LOVE

"I have asked you, I have directed you, as your Mother, to retire--retire from your world that has been given to Satan. You must earn your daily bread by living in the world, but you must not become of the world. Your children must be guided with a strong discipline and love. But this love must be coming from the light, my children, for so few cry love, and they have lost the true meaning of love. For love is your God the Father in Heaven." *Our Lady, September 7, 1976; 1972 Source:* <u>http://www.tldm.org-</u> *Copyright © These Last Days Ministries, Inc. 1998 - 2002 all rights reserved.*

Case Study #3

Children are being raised with a sense of entitlement, and no moral fiber, nor the necessary allure for life. It's sad when hearing a mother say their child can handle money extremely well as if it's a badge of honor. Yet, they have no accountability. Why would anyone brag about their child handling money that's not theirs (earned) to handle? The child is being given money or you put the child on your bank account with full access to your funds. **Are you kidding me?**

In this particular study, it reminds me of a young woman that was twenty-two years old, who has been in two different colleges and could not cut it. You as a parent removed her after paying hundreds and thousands of dollars. Can you make that decision after reading this case study? Did this child ever have the right stuff before going to college? Or was she missing several ingredients?

Okay, another bright idea, she drops out of college and you buy this same child a brand new car that most adults could not afford to drive. She now has transportation to run out on "booty calls" at the boyfriend's house. **Are you kidding me?!**

The next bright idea was to give her an American Express gold card. You want to make sure she has that card for emergencies. However, her spending is beyond control on herself, the boyfriend, as well as others having big parties on your dime. So far what has this child been taught?

DO NOT FALL DOWN

Do not fall down in your job as a parent, for you will also be held responsible for the condition of your children's souls when they are brought to us." - *Our Lady, February 11, 1971.*

Girlfriend, please, I know, I know, what else could be done to hinder this child's ambition to succeed in life? Well here we go again! Can you image this mom came up with another bright idea to give this twenty-two year old daughter some responsibility. A job in her daddy's business emptying a few trash cans. This will of course teach her some accountability. She may earn a paycheck each week so she can learn the value of money. She shows up or not, work or not, and still gets paid that same $400 a week. **Are you kidding me?**

Please correct me if I'm wrong, but where is the lesson in that? Have we set the standard for this twenty- two year old who has never finished anything that she can work when she wants to plus get paid?

This girl is being set up for failure, because when she is out in the real world her parent expectations maybe far less than the expectation of others. Of course this child is still not paying any bills at all out of the $400 per week salary. Most adults break their backs to earn over an eight hours work day.

Sister girl is paying her daughters cell phone bill, car note, automobile insurance, taxes, registration, doctor's bills, food each week, shoes and clothes. And this child just won't clean her room. Did I leave anything out? You're puzzled, and so am I because you don't understand why you can't get her to do anything except spend money. Oh yeah, I forgot, she of course runs to the boyfriend's house for "booty calls". **Are you kidding me?**

Imagine one day this young lady goes into your bank account and "steals" $300.00, but you don't consider it stealing because it's your child. You curse her out, call her names, and tell her in no uncertain terms the repercussions of her actions. Finally, guess what, a few days pass, and "nothing". **Are you kidding me?** Well, let's see the definition of stealing: pocketing, pinching, shoplifting, appropriation, embezzlement, thieving etc…

What's the next lesson being taught to this young lady? She can take what does not belong to her, with no consequence.

In this millennium are there no consequences or accountability for our children's actions at all.

This is a young lady who unfortunately, may not make it to the next level of life without mommy or daddy. We must pray to God nothing will happen to them or this kid will be on skid row. It's not simply the money, it's the fact that no responsibility or accountability is being taught.

WHY?

1. You tell this child each and every week that you are going to take the car back, but you never do. *Are you kidding me?*
2. You tell this child you're going to take the American express card back, but you never do. *Are you kidding me?*
3. You tell this child you're going to put her out of your house, but you never do. *Are you kidding me?*
4. Then one day after an argument with the child she tells you, I'm not going anywhere this is my house.

Are you kidding ....me!

When did the house that you work for become the twenty-two year old child's house? Did you die and your ghost is having this conversation with this child at this moment? I know, did you sign a deed over to this child? No, you are dead and she got the house from your will. "Oh no" did the probate court assign the house to her, while you were still alive? Please let me know when this house transferred to this child (22 years old), who's telling you she is not getting out of your house.

Maybe, you should get out or ask this child for permission to stay in your own house. I continue to call this young lady a child, because she has not really been taught how to be a responsible young woman. **<u>Again, are you listening,</u>** are you dead yet, or did you sign the deed to the house to this child? The child continues to be disrespectful to you and the household *(demanding, yelling, and slamming doors),* but you continue to give and give to this child. What do you think, magically that this child is going to wake up one day with a new found respect for you and the world?

"Not"! Sorry, this chapter is not just for girls.

ENTITLED FAVORITE CHILD

Case Study #4 ~ **Gail's Story!**

I knew a woman that had two boys. I could not understand why one of the boys was treated like King Tut and the other like a step child. It was astounding, watching these boys grow up into manhood. This woman jumped through hoops to get these boys through school. Mr. King Tut was supposed to be a basketball superstar. The other one, she felt would not be on the same level with his brother. **Are you kidding me?**

Consciously or not she was investing into this one kid and not the other. Big mistake. He was going to be her knight in shining armor and buy his mother this big house one day with his basketball talent. The problem with this situation was that this boy was disrespectful, talked back to her, told her what he was going to do, and when. **Are you kidding**

me? He did things to his mother during the time she was divorcing his dad, he should have never done.

Interestingly, one day I went to her house and her son was sleep. She opens the door and puts her finger to her lips, signifying I needed to be quiet. This was a sixteen year old kid, sleep in the early afternoon on a Saturday. Shouldn't he be cutting the grass or raking the yard. She notified me that he does not like it when you wake him up with noise.

Are you kidding me? Is it just me? Let me get this straight. This is a sixteen year old kid, living, eating, and sleeping in your house, where you pay all the bills, and you must be quiet so you don't disturb him. Yeah, right! He does not pay any bills, do any housework, clean his room, the bathroom, or cut the grass.

Fast forward. Several years passed and she continued to be extremely hard on the other son. He had to work around the house and perform other tasks for people to earn money to pay for the extra things he wanted. King Tut, had a car. He did not have to pay for any repairs or gas. The other son, could not drive unless he paid the cost associated with his car.

Inside myself, I knew she really did not realize it but King Tut is going to be a disappointment to her. While the other son probably would be successful. I remember getting into a heated debate with her concerning King Tut. He had a tendency to take advantage of people. He would also lie. Instead of her telling him that he was wrong, she continued to take his side, no matter what. **Are you kidding me?**

It was sad but now the younger son had enough and was now starting to copy the behavior of King Tut. Fortunately, all of this negative behavior was not embedded into him as it was in King Tut. Unfortunately, the argument got out of control. I said, "Your boys will never amount to anything in life." Big mistake. Our friendship ended. Sorry, some mothers will not allow the assistance of a village to raise her child.

Over the next several years, King Tut barely kept his grades up. He slept around and did pretty much whatever he wanted. He was the star of his high school basketball team, on a fast track to college. The problem with this situation was he really did not earn the grades he needed to go to college.

This is another kid who should never have gone to college because his grade point average (GPA) was low. He could not graduate on time to get his full ride scholarship. As always, his mom wanted to help him. This woman sprang into action. She went to the school, and cajoled coaches and teachers into changing his grades *(he did not earn),* to meet the GPA requirements he needed to be eligible. **Are you really….kidding me!**

So, what lesson did he learn? That's it was okay to lie, cheat, and steal grades to get the scholarship for college. I know most people may not think this is a big deal, but it builds character and values for the future. The funny thing was that this woman had the nerve to always talk about GOD and religion.

THE LESSONS WE TEACH OUR CHILD WITH THE UNSPOKEN WORD!

I bet you can guess what happened, to this young man who went to college. He lost his full scholarship because he could not maintain his grades. King Tut continued to complain about the coaches being too hard on him and he got kicked out for smoking weed. Then of course according to her, it was the coaches and schools that did not like her son and she transferred him to another school. **Are you kidding me?**

Well, the original school should not be too upset because the second school did not fare any better. He got kicked out again for smoking weed as well. When will it be that the child is the real problem? After all he's the common denominator. Did she give her child the right formula growing up? Obviously she can't bake a cake either. They all can't be wrong and he's always right.

Now he has several children, unmarried to the girl with no job living with his parents. Unfortunately, instead of King Tut having riches of gold, this woman created a male monster at the age of twenty-three with no moral values. He is loose on this world to destroy another young woman's life.

Yes, it takes to two make a baby at a young age and not have the financial means to take care of it. However, better moral values and character would have made a world of difference. He has no financial stability, home of his own, and need his parents to help feed him, the girlfriend, and grandchildren.

It's almost comical how I tried to tell my friend that her son was not learning any respect or responsibility. She really got upset at me and of course we do not talk to this day. A friendship that is missed beyond words!

I know it is often ill-advised for someone to share negative feedback about one's child. What parent wants to hear it; even if it is beneficial? The advice I gave was not empty advice I was handing down. She knew I had already raised two boys and I to, had made some of the same mistakes time and again by giving my boys too much without accountability. Looking back, I wish I could change some things with my boys. Maybe their lives would have been different.

Somehow, it was like looking through a looking glass of the future. I could really see from the outside looking in. I loved and cared for her, as well as her boys. She really did not care for my comments.

Ladies, it's about deposits and withdrawals!

If you make good deposits now into your children, someday they will have good withdrawals and success in life. For some reason, if you are not careful, boys learn early on how to charm the pants off their moms; not in an incest way.

As Phaedra Parks would say "They'll blow smoke up your butt with a bubble-blower if they have to, especially when they're dealing with a lady".

Unfortunately, this is doubly true when boys are trying to get their way with their moms. Is it at this time in a young man's life he learns how to get over and manipulate women from their own mothers. Helping her son, lie, cheat, and steal to get into a college that boy really did not earn was a big blunder. He had the attitude that everything was easy and just like his mom, everyone would just hand him everything on a silver platter with no accountability.

My saving grace was that when my son was at that point early in life and he did not want to listen, when he felt he wanted to be disrespectful to me, he was out. Yes, I mean out of my house. If you want to act like a grown adult, then you need to have those grown up responsibilities and take care of yourself. I was not going to allow a child of mine to disrespect me in my house where I pay the bills. I also was not going to give him a sense of entitlement. We may not always agree, and it killed me to put my eighteen year old son out. None the less, he has owned two homes, pays his own bills, and gave me four wonderful grandchildren.

So what is this sense of entitlement being bred into our children that keeps them from really being a positive, productive person in our society? I know, I know, you can try your best to give your child all the right stuff and some- thing happens to that child. Is it your fault? Maybe not. Are you having problems baking a cake too? Were you taught the correct use of a measurement cup to bake that perfect cake? However, nothing is promised to us in this world and we need to raise our children with the understand- ing that the world owes them nothing. Every cup of coffee cost something.

SO MUCH DISCORD, "Children of the world, there is so much discord among families. There is so much deteriora- tion among families. This is not a good sign. The family unit must be together under the true sign of the living God. Mothers and fathers have a great responsibility for their children. You who spend your hours, so few upon earth, giving your children their bodily delights, their materialistic wishes and pleasures, while their souls are starving and they are being led on the path that will take them farther from the Kingdom. Sin, the darkest of sins, is being committed in the homes. What example as parents are you showing to your children?" - *St. Joseph, December 30, 1972.*

Should we all not want more for our children generation to generation, where characteristic building should be a must? As in case study #3, this same woman can't really impart character and morals to her daughter because she really had none. Can you imagine just for one moment that this woman never married her daughter's father, but has lived in a common law situation since this child was born? That was not the only issue. This woman met this man by taking this man from his wife and child of a previous marriage. **Are you kidding me…?**

Sister to sister, is it okay in today's society to destroy a family unit for self-interest? She befriends her girlfriend and finally took her girlfriends husband, got pregnant and set up house. I always tell people to be careful what you wish for because the sins of the father are passed onto the son. The same holds for women. The sins of the mother are being passed on to the daughter.

You grow up in life and you wonder what's wrong with this child. Why is she or he like this, and you have no earthly idea? Maybe it had nothing to do with earth, but the sins you placed before GOD. You began to pray to GOD because you really don't understand why so many bad things are happening to you and your family. Then this child continues to watch her mother over the years be selfish and self-centered.

To go to any extreme to get what she wants, as when she took another woman's husband. Now this mother is wondering how she raised such a selfish daughter. The act is in the doing and not in the saying. You can preach all day to your child but that child is ultimately watching what you are doing. That's the strongest lesson they learn.

Remember when you were growing up some mothers would say, "Do as I say, but not as I do." That never worked, because you had children who became drunks, just like their father or mother. The parents would drink liquor and tell their children, I don't want to ever catch you drinking. However that never stops anyone from drinking and getting drunk. You have some parents who will lie to get their children out of a DUI, knowing this child was drinking and driving. Never mind that this child could have killed themselves and others as well.

Parents we should live more by "practicing what we preach". I do not drink alcohol, use drugs nor do I smoke cigarettes, so if any of my children took up those habits, it would not be something they could say they learned from their mother.

FIRMNESS IS NEEDED! "I wish that all fathers of households stand forth and practice their role. They will use the rod and not permit their children to go astray.

Firmness is needed in your world that is filled with laxity, permissiveness, and degradation. "Your children have been misled by many who shall answer to the Father. As teachers they have failed in their role. Therefore, as parents you must succeed in yours." - *St. Joseph, March 18, 1973.* *Source:* http://www.tldm.org- *Copyright © These Last Days Ministries, Inc. 1998 - 2002 all rights reserved.*

As Phaedra Parks from the Atlanta Housewives would say, "Every saint has a past and every sinner has a future." This means, it's never too late to change your world around. It's never too late to build morals and character and impart those objects to our children.

IS FIRM Man has lost his purity. All parents must guard the children's souls. Be firm with your children. The fashions grieve all Heaven.

"The time is short, so you must make reparation now, and learn to recognize the signs. You must be guided by the light. The Holy Spirit will always be with you. Remain close to My Son. So many will be lost." - *Our Lady, August 5, 1970.* I say to you do you want your child to be one of the lost ones in life.

"The future of humanity passes by way of the family." - Pope John Paul II, November 22, 1981

Chapter 4 – Why do we give it away?

It's all so astonishing how some women give it away for free. *"Why buy the cow, when you are getting the milk for fee"*. What happened to those good old days of let's stay a virgin until you get married?

In Case Study #5

It's funny, I was talking to a mother, who was telling me that her daughter was moving to another state with her boyfriend. I asked if they were getting married and she said "God, no!" As if the word marriage was dirty. **Are you kidding me?** She elaborated on how she really wanted her daughter to live with him first to try it out. So this mother is promoting her daughter with support and encouragement of giving away the cookies for free.

She justified her position by serving me up propaganda about divorce being difficult, and it would be better for her daughter not to be married until she got to know him. However, it's okay to give away the cookies to someone you don't know yet. All I could think was that she had a lot of baggage that she was passing on to her daughter. She continued her rhetorical propaganda by further inserting that it would be easier for her daughter to walk away, if they were not married.

Hum… really **are you kidding me**. Have we as people traded morals and commitment for the fear of what may or may not happen down the road. Suppose they live together for four years, then they decide to get married and six months later they got divorced. Why? What happened? I have seen it time and time again. It's really not only the piece of paper you get with the marriage, it's your mind set, your essence, and soul you are about to share on the highest level of intimacy.

For some reason people that are not married, have those I can walk away attitude.   I personally believe that marry people try harder. They have a bond and can't just walk away from their marriage. As I stated generational lessons are very hard to break. So what lesson has this mother taught her daughter that she will no doubt teach, her daughter?   Is this the legacy we want for our children, and our children's, children.

I remember when I was growing up how some young women would tease other women. Calling them whore or prostitute for getting paid to have sex with men. What was so amazing was how they separated themselves from these so called whores. Why? So, you have a prostitute who gets paid fifty dollars for giving a man oral pleasure.

Then you have women who are dating what they believe to be great guys on a regular. Yes, they are sexually active and she wants to get her hair and nails done this week. She knows, this week she needs to be extra special to her man, She goes to his house on Friday and cooks him dinner, washes his clothes, cleans his house, and she sexes him up.

Are you kidding me? Sister Girl knows this is her ticket to the salon.

Saturday morning, they have sex again and he gives her fifty dollars, then drops her off at the salon, and picks her up. Now, do you really have blinders on, and who do you think got the better deal? Do you think the prostitute who got the fifty dollars for sexual favors that took ten to fifteen minutes and sent her john packing? Or, the girlfriend who spent twenty four hours as a cook, maid, and sex toy at approximately two dollars and eight cents per hour? **ARE YOU KIDDING ME?**

Come on girlfriend stop it. We have all "prostituted" ourselves at one time or another to get what we wanted. Stop using words that cut your sister's soul, like tramp, whore etc... We just don't call it that because we are not trading sexual favors every fifteen minutes. Do you really know what the word whore means? ***Whore***, *an offensive term for somebody who is regarded as willing to set aside principles or personal integrity in order to obtain something, usually for self-motives.*

Maybe it was not money, but a new stove, fur coat, diamond ring. Think about it. It's all the same. You are performing a service to get something out of your man for self-motives. I guess the other woman is a whore because she's engaging in this behavior with different men. I see, so when you give away the cookies, break up with that guy, then date another guy, give away the cookies, break up with that guy, then date another guy and give away the cookies, and so on and so on. Is that okay? **Are you kidding me...?**

Let's see you're now on guy number twelve, but you are not a whore because "what" he's not putting cash in your hand or on the nightstand each and every time you go down town. Again, read the definition of **Whore**, *an offensive term for somebody who is regarded as willing to set aside principles or personal integrity in order to obtain something, usually for self-motives.*

I would like to leave you with this "wisdom," each and every time you have sex with a man, whore, prostitute or not, you leave a piece of your soul "your essence" behind. Why do you think that some women who are prostitutes or have multiple partners may drink or use drugs to get through it? A piece of them is being left behind. They get high to block it out because the man that they are with does not give love, share their own essence, and transcend power to empower them.

When you're in a truly loving, non-abusive committed relationship, the giving of essence is shared and flows both ways and both parties are satisfied and empowered. If you find that you are not in that wholesome relationship than you will find comfort in **Psalm 37:4** "Delight in the Lord, and he will give thee the requests of thy heart." Not all relationships are blessed by the Lord. Maybe you need to wait on Him to bring you that special man in our life. A special love which is unconditional and bless by GOD.

*C*hapter **5** – **L**iar, Liar pants on fire

What is it? He lies and lies and tells you more lies over and over and over again. You continue to believe this man, why? Do you think that rolling pin is made of gold, platinum steel or what? Is his rolling pin more powerful than your pie? Men tend to rule with their brains regarding their heart, however sometimes the small head takes control over the big head and never thinks about the consequences until the action is over.

So what is our excuse? Are we the same, do we just think about the lust of it all and give away our cookies to any big rolling pin that drops his pants? Are we that gullible to a feeling that usually last all but five minutes to climax? Again, what is it? **Are you kidding me?**

Are you screaming in bed telling your man he is the best and to get it big daddy? When in your head you're saying, "hurry up and get off me?"

Can you tell me what this is about with these relationships based on lies? Is that why people cheat, both men and women? It's really not about the love, but the lust of that old so good feeling over and over again. It may be the worst drug addiction of them all, greater than heroin, cocaine or even crack-cocaine. A feeling of endorphin rush that keeps calling your name over and over again.

"**Endorphins** *("endogenous morphine") are <u>endogenous</u> <u>opioid</u> <u>peptides</u> that function as <u>neurotransmitters</u>. They are produced by the* *pituitary gland* and the *hypothalamus* in *vertebrates* during *exercise*, *excitement*, *pain*, *consumption of spicy food*, *love* and *orgasm*, and they resemble the *opiates* in their abilities to produce *analgesia* and a feeling of well-being".

An addiction is so strong you can't fight the taste of getting that feeling over and over again. So you cheat on your mate to find that feeling. You continue to lie and cheat to get it. What is it about some of us that can control the feeling of lust and the true love for our partner really over takes the power of lust and prevents us from cheating on our mates? Is it like that drug addiction behavior, that some are prone to and some not so much. Do we really know what drives people to become liars?

It's been my experience over the last fifty six years on this earth that some women want to be lied to over and over again. Some women prefer to accept the lie than the truth. If a man came to you and said, "Look honey, I love you and I love Sally down the street. I want to taste a slice of both yours and Sally's sweet potato pies. Would you continue to develop a relationship with this man? What would you say? **"ARE YOU KIDDING ME"!** That answer most likely would be no. You would contend that you will not share your man with another woman.

If this man came to you and said, "I love you and I don't love Sally and we are just friends. We don't have sex and I deserve to have friends outside of our relationship." Somehow you know down in the pit of your stomach that he is not only getting slices of Sally's pie but tasting your sweet potato pie every chance he gets. Would you still continue to see this man? Yes, because you want to believe him even

56

though you know he is having a relationship with both you and Sally.

Six months later you actually caught him tasting a slice of Sally's pie. You call him a liar. He comes to you and he says, "I don't love Sally, I love you and I will not see Sally anymore." Of course you love your man and you continue the relationship with him because you want to believe him. You continue this relationship with this man and during the next year, your relationship continues to get rocky and he does not spend the quality time with you as he did before.

When he comes around he's normally too tired and he wants to argue to get out of the house. You continue in this relationship because you love your man but deep down in your gut you have a feeling he is seeing this other woman, Sally. Again, you catch him with her. He tells you that he was just helping her move furniture, because they are just friends. You continue this relationship with this man and two years has passed. Now you find out that Sally is pregnant with his baby. **Are you kidding me?**

You stay because he tells you it was a mistake and he really loves you and not Sally. Why do you stay? Because you have two years invested into this man and now you're upset because he's a liar? What part of this relationship are you not sharing with this man and other women? You are sharing this man with Sally but you know you would not be in this relationship with this man if he told you the truth from day one. So it's his fault?

Are you kidding me? You knew your man was eating sweet potato pie at Sally's house. You wanted to pretend he was not. In your mind as long as he was lying to you the story was true that "he loves you and not Sally". You saw all the "red flags" and you continued with this man in this relationship.

Now you are in a relationship, sharing your man with another woman. You are really upset, now this woman has one up on you because she switch from sweet potato pie to cake baking. In fact, she has a cake baking in her oven. She is having his baby! You continue to stay with this man because you love him. What happened to your self-image? Is it tied to his soul? Why would you continue in any relationship sharing a man and much worst with a man that has lied to you over and over again? **Are you kidding me?**

JUST IMAGINE

I know this may be a hard pill to swallow. Perhaps we are teaching our sweet innocent boys at an early age how to be liars. They in turn use what we taught to get what they want from women? Are we the blame? Does the buck stop here? Are we doing such a great job as moms teaching our boys unconsciously deep in the psyche to become liars far below our consciousness? Oh no, of course not, we would never admit, that we are doing that, especially on purpose.

Let's just think about it! You have a young boy at six years old and he's misbehaving as most boys do at his age. Now, he's in trouble and you say tell me the truth, no matter what you will not get into trouble. He tells you _not_ the truth, but what he thinks you want to hear.

This is a whopping story coming from the mouth of this six year old boy and you're in such disbelief. Not because he's lying to you but that he's smart enough to come up with such a story. You know he is lying to you but the lie is so good you can't believe such a great lie.

You give him a big kiss, no punishment and let him go on about his way. You tell all your family, and friends this great story about your son being smart enough to conjure up this lie. He hears you telling the story over and over again. Now, everyone in the family continues to kiss and hug him stating "he's such a smart little boy."

What did you just teach him? You decide!

Was that his very first lesson in lying to get out of any type of punishment or spanking? I can guarantee that will not be his only performance of lying.

Ladies, are we sleeping with the enemy who learned the skill of lying from a very young age. Men who are liars have had a lot of practice. Do you really believe they will change because you think you have magic cookies? **Are you Kidding Me?**

Know your worth in life and demand that worth from the man you are with, so you both can have a loving caring relationship for years to come.

Chapter **6** – **H**e did not change, I did?

It's amusing how when a woman meets a man she will confess to herself that she and he are falling in love. However, she does not like this or that about this man. The women will look over his short coming's believing, if he loves her, he will change or I'm woman enough to change those bad habits.

What happens when you're dating and you just know that your man loves you and you love him? He starts out loving you and can't keep his hands off you and pays you that attention that no man has ever paid you before? You think he must really love you, he wants to spend every day, every moment of that day he can with you. You have cut off your BFF, family and friends, plus stop doing other activities because your man wants you all to himself.

So of course you know he worships the ground you walk on. You can't help but fall in love with this man. Then you give up the cookies and all of the sudden, after a short time, the tides change. You really don't understand why, because you have been doing everything for this man, loving him giving him the best sex of his life "you think", so you don't understand. Your man begins to lie to you, minor little tiny lies but they are lies none the less.

He has to play basketball with his friend, so he can't come over today. He's got to do something for his mom, so he can't come over today. Now, you don't know what is going on because the attention that he exhibited *(to put on an exhibition or performance)* toward you in the beginning is gone. He is no longer all over you. You believe he still loves you, but the interest is fading and you don't know why. You ask him, "what's going on baby, do you not love me the same anymore?" He reassures you by taking you to bed and making love to you. He makes sure to say, "I love you," ever so gentle.

You believe him and he starts to pay a little more attention but nothing like before. You continue to isolate yourself from your BFF, family, and friends to jump thru hoops for this man. You're like a little junkie. You just don't know that this man has been giving you heavy doses of something that parallels heroin shots, himself. Now you're hooked and ted to his sole.

He no longer has a need to spend the time he used to spend with you because, you are hooked. You are not going anywhere and if he pulls away, you will chase him for your next shot. He knows that you're so in love with him that his effort level toward this relationship does not need to be the same as yours. He knows he's got you, because you changed your entire life to be with him. Now you love and want him more than he loves and wants you. **Are you kidding me?**

It's been about five months into this relationship and he continues with the little lies that are now turning into big lies. You continue in this relationship looking for that feeling of that first shot, that first high that first shot gave you in the very beginning. You are chasing this dream of what was.

You don't understand why it's not the same. What you fail to realize is, that you're chasing "lust" not love.

It's just like eating a piece of chocolate and you get that rush and you continue to eat chocolate, but you need more chocolate to get that same rush. Then one day, you don't want the chocolate anymore and you need a break from the chocolate because you're sick of the chocolate at this point. Men are on the same concept, they detach easier than women, you have given him too much chocolate *(white or dark)* and he now needs a break.

However, you're now chasing him and he's running because your obsession is now overwhelming and he must get away. You find yourself blowing up his phone, and maybe following him in your car just to see where he's going or if he's telling you the truth. He does not want to hurt the relationship or your feelings so he begins to lie to get away. This is the problem, when you first start out a relationship; you're in lust with the person, not in love so remember that.

How can you be in love with someone you hardly know at all? You both see each other's physical appearance and you both know you want each other. I know as women, we like to pretend it's not the physical, when in fact it's exactly that appearance that will attract us to that man initially. The second part of the problem is that you cut off your BFF, friends and family to consume this man.

You changed everything about yourself, you have given up your self-worth, and your own identity to be with this man. Why? What you fail to realize is that he was falling in love with you, the person you were and now you have changed.

Why should he continue to love you the same. You have really changed and not him! You as a woman need to maintain, your own space, your own identity, keep your BFF, family, and friends, just like he needs his space, you need yours. If, in fact it is true love, over the test of time eventually he will put a ring on it. If not, move on!

Women, listen up, have you not heard the phrase "you cannot raise grown folks over again"? Then why is it that you are continually trying to re-raise men. When you meet a man and he's using drugs, he's not going to stop. More than likely you will start using. If, you meet a man that sleeps around, he's not going to stop. More than likely you are going to give yourself hard aches trying to stop him.

If you meet a man that's into threesomes, he's not going to stop. If you meet a man, that loves to slip through the back door, before you know it, you will be opening the door and letting him in. If you meet a man that is looking for a sugar momma and wants you to pay the bills, he's not going to change. If you meet a man that hangs out in the street he is not going to stop.

When I say, he's not going to stop, what I mean is permanently stop negative behavior. Yes, to get you emotionally attached to him, he will stop for a short time period. This is to his benefit, because he knows you don't like certain things and he knows that if he shows you that he is bending to your way you will continue to move the relationship toward an emotional commitment.

Now you are hooked, just like that a little junkie continually waiting for another shot of heroin *(from that rolling pin you come to know so well)* and all along, you thought you were changing him. Again, I ask did he change or did you? How much of your essence and self-worth was given away for the sake of this relationship with this man?

Chapter 7 – Women in the Media
(Real life vs. Fiction)

Women really should not get caught up in fictional and television personalities. What is it about when a television show portrays women, who continue to run behind men demanding a wedding ring of marriage? It's clear when a man does not want to marry you. If he did you would already have a ring. The Atlanta House Wives franchise showed segments that was in very poor taste for Ms. USA. Kenya Moore. She should be a "Strong" beautiful, successful woman with wealth and money. Yet she's constantly belittled with very low self-image regarding man issues.

Are we being portrayed in the media wrongly or is the media portraying what we are in real life? To continue to beg for a ring, over and over again on national television, when it's abundantly clear, her love interest is not ready for marriage. I have watched this show season, after season with the women and men in their lives. Never have I ever seen such low self-image being portrayed in a woman running after a man, on national television, which can impact very young impressionable young women.

To date, Kenya has still not experienced enough disrespect and humiliation, so they give her more. In one show, Kenya comes off vacation, where her man is not that into her and of course, she wants to know why. So, she takes her man fishing, just the place where he would be relaxed and ready to open up to her about his feelings.

Are you kidding me? He shows up in white short pants and white sneakers, and clearly he is not going fishing for real. Kenya cast her fishing line and it gets caught up in the bank and he's telling her to go get her own hook out of the water. Then to add icing on that cake with continual disrespectful behavior and facial expression, she's demanding to know why he did not try to have sex with her in the shower.

After all, she's Miss USA, beautiful, and butt naked, so of course he must be gay according to Kenya. He's now saying, "I don't need to tell you when it's time to do something." Come on! The sad thing is that this woman continues to cry to others, making excuses for the man, but he's a great father, he's kind, and he loves or maybe you're thinking of that word "lust"... He may be a great dad, he maybe kind, but not to you and he may be the most loving man in the world for some other woman.

So it's only when he's on camera he's a prick to this woman. It is clear Kenya really did not have "the talk" or she was talking about marriage and he's talking about something else. Somewhere there is miscommunication going on with this man or he's not that into you. Oh, I know when the rolling pin is at attention he's really into you. That's not love, but "L U S T".

My Sisters, we need to understand that these reality shows are for entertainment and not true form. We also need to understand that love is unselfish loyalty and benevolent concern for the good of another. Was he really concerned and being unselfish when he sent his woman into the water to fetch your own fish hook? No, he was more concern about those white sneakers. Lust, is something that does not belong to you, not really.

The more I watch these realities shows, I am praying this is really a bad script written for television to boost ratings. However, women should not be betrayed in a character with such extreme low self-image. Kenya stated time and time again that she is a part of history and that title of Miss USA 1993 represents women around the world in the best possible light, especially to young women. That is not a role "Kenya Moore" should have accepted or played being a part of history, in which she aligned herself with Presidents.

I really do not understand why she played television roles that would portray her as a desperate woman who want a man to marry her like yesterday and pot a baby in the oven. Another week has gone by and I don't know if Kenya really found self-image or did the producers of the show realize how bad it look to have Miss. USA continue to beg this man for a ring to marry her. Because she's in her forties, she must get pregnant. Either way, I was glad that display of begging was over because it showed her in very poor taste.

Kenya had the nerve to get upset because at the Bailey Agency, a young lady was showing vagina and butt crack. However, she did not get upset over her own behavior. **Are you kidding me?** Then to make matters worse, she shows up for a charity for women naked again with her butt cheeks hanging out. So what example was she trying to show the young women of America being she's a part of history?

When Phaedra was on the beach or on vacation in Anguilla she showed up with a bathing suit and fishnet outfit, more than what I would wear but they were on the beach. We all understand that Kenya was trying to make a point with Phaedra, but that was not the time and place. Additionally, as Miss USA, it was in poor taste and very inappropriate, she's a role model to women all over the world. Yeah, right! **Are you kidding me, Miss USA?**

Ladies do you believe that any young woman should model themselves after a Miss USA who portrays a desperate woman with very low self-worth or self-image? She can say whatever she likes, claiming it was not an act, and she was in love with Walter. It was clear that he knew nothing about any marriage. If what Kenya said was true, Miss USA can be a fool as well. The lesson here is that you really need to get to know the man, ask the hard questions. Find out what he wants for his future and make sure it's you, or don't waste your time.

Case Study #6 ~ porn movies

I interviewed a young lady in the porn industry. If what she stated to me is true, the movie industry really needs to be addressed. It appears to be driving some women in the wrong direction. It's sad when women watch porn movies and believe the sex scenes being portrayed. **Are you kidding me?** She stated that they put the biggest guys with the smallest women to enlarge his rolling pin. The camera does the rest to make it appear he's twenty feet long.

She continued to tell me how they splice the scenes

together. Some women are allowing themselves to be passed from man to man. Finding themselves into three ways sexual escapades. Women need to understand, when they get into anything whether its sex or drugs, it's an evolution. You are slowly being moved toward that direction under the pretense of money or love by a man.

Again, you are being introduced to this way of life by a man who really does not care for you in such a way that demonstrates love. In the beginning you are not into this type of behavior. Now your man is asking you to watch these movies with him.

The more you are together, he wants to watch these movies. Then he's trying to play round with your backdoor and you tell him to stop. You continue to tell him you don't want to do that and he continues to tell you that he wants to love all of you. He is now investing all of his time into you, telling you he would not do anything to hurt you and how much he loves you.

One day he has his friends over to the house and in the group are other women *(shame on your sisters)* who are opening the back door. I say shame on your sisters, because they are opening the door not of their own free will. They are helping a man pressure and turn another woman out. You do not want to open the backdoor, but the other women are pushing. It's very unfortunate but it happens more than you know that other women help men turn out other women whether it's drugs or sex. Why it is that men have a code among men and women's code will go out the window when you throw a man in the mix?

After the pushing and pulling by the other women, he wants you to watch porn movies. You really don't want to watch especially in front of his friends. The other women again, start to talk about how it's really no big deal.

He's being sweet to you and telling you in your ear to go with if you love him. **Are you kidding me?** So you stay, because you love this man and now watching the movies everyone start having relations. This happens several more times and you are not opening the backdoor yet.

One day all the friends show up again. Everyone is watching the movies. All of a sudden, you find yourself now being passed around to his friends. You can't believe this is happening. Your man keeps coming back to you saying he loves you and he wants to enter the backdoor. Finally, you give in. Afterward, he rewards you with an alcoholic beverage to numb the physical and emotional pain. **Are you kidding me?**

Note: I am not passing judgment on anyone's sexual activities between two consenting adults. However, this chapter is inserted for those who do not partake and are being seduce into this way of life under the pretense of love.

Now that you have been turned out, his interest in you appears to be gone. When you tell him you're leaving because he does not love you anymore he has his way with you to get you to stay.

SISTERS ARE YOU BEING TURNED OUT?

Are you missing several ingredients in your formula to allow this man to turn you out? Women who are prostitutes or party girls don't wake up one day and decide I want to be that when I grow up. **Are you kidding me?**

It's a succession of making the wrong choices, and not saying "no" when a door of darkness opens and jumps into their path. I know you believed he loved you, but you forgot the most important part that was you *didn't* love yourself. That's what led you to the path where you really did not want to be.

Just think of it this way, it starts with a slice of cake that you really don't want to eat. Someone cajoles you to just take a bite. You take a little bite and say you don't really want any more. They persuade you to take another bite. You take another bite for a bigger taste. In your mind you are saying, "Well, I already took two bites so I ought to eat the rest of the cake." You eat the rest of the cake. Now you're sorry you open that door because you ate something you really did not want.

You are kicking yourself because you really don't understand how you let someone else talk you into eating the cake. It becomes much more than about the cake. You begin to question your strength. You might say this is a poor parallel from sex to a piece of cake, but is it.

It is the same concept? You were not able to say "no", whether it's a piece of cake or sex. Someone else was forcing you to eat cake or force you into having backdoor sex with multiple partners.

Now, don't get me wrong, if you and your man love porn movies or going in the backdoor, that's between you and him. However, it becomes a problem when you are not into the same type of sexual activities as your man and you are being pushed beyond your comfort zone...

If he's trying to manipulate you by saying, "If you love me you will do this." You really could say **are you kidding me**, if you love me you will not force sexual activities beyond my comfort zone.

Perhaps you succumbed to his will because he threatened to break up with you. You're terrified he's going to dump you for the other woman. Guess what? He already dumped you the minute he gave you to his friends. The best thing you can do for yourself is to let him go. Believe me, you will find someone down the road that will really love you and respect your sexual boundaries.

Chapter 8 – Does it matter?
Young vs. Old "G"

I hear a lot of women say that they have an old "G". They don't have the care and concerns you have with young "G's". **Are you kidding** me? I would not bet on it. I have seen some very old "G's" go buck wild, because they run up on some young thing that will go down south. Giving him something you won't or that he has not experienced. Whether your man is young or old, there are ten personality traits women should avoid in selecting a man. If you are currently in one of those relationships with these men, "RUN" to the nearest exit. Don't walk!

Women should avoid these Ten Personality traits in Men

1) **"Married Men" As** Ne Ne Leakes would say, *"Close your legs to married men"*- Why is it that women feel that when they meet a married man, she would be so much better for that man than his current wife or girlfriend *(common law)*. Why, because you think you have a better understanding of him and he is being so misunderstood by his mate? Or, because you got the cookies to die for and no other woman can lay it down like you can? Believe me when I tell you that cookies are cookies and pie is pie, ask any man. So what's the attraction that demands that you acquire this unavailable man? We know exactly why he

wants you, but why do you want him? It will never be a satisfying relationship because he can't give you the 100% attention that you deserve. He's taken! Why degrade yourself by not knowing your worth. Do you not want a man that can give you a 100% relationship without sharing him with someone else? Say he decides to leave his wife or girlfriend. Be careful what you ask for. How you got that man is how that relationship will end. Women of the world, when another woman takes your man, let him go. She did you a gigantic favor. That man has a traveling spirit. When she finds that same man she took from you, that supposed to love her so much is now cheating, she should have *"No Complaints"*. And, surprise, surprise she has the nerve to get distressed over the fact that he's now cheating on her.

2) **"Bad Boy"** - What is it about these bad boys that are so attractive to women? You want that man you think you can use for money and relations. Eventually, you find that you are the one being used. You want that three strikes you're out felon. Oh by the way, I must have that dirty thug on the street. Why do you put yourself in a position to be pimped out? You know for a fact that sooner or later you will become involved with criminal activity. If not that, he's passing you around like a groupie to other men to perform sexual favors for money. So what part of this do you not get? Why is this continual reoccurrence with women?

3) **"God's Gift to Woman Man"** - This type of man is what you would call a "ladies man". He knows his stuff don't stink and he can be a very frustrating man to deal with. He is always being surrounded with

women telling him he's the cat's meow. This type of man is not good around other men, so they stick to the woman. They need to have their ego consistently stroked. This man will always be a cheating man because he is always looking for the next young thing.

4) **"Weak Men"** - These men are very easily intimidated by strong women and normally welcome third party interference to fight his battles. This man is usually psychologically and emotionally weak in nature. He simply cannot handle his own situation and will never be able to handle himself. He will not be a protector of you or himself and will usually get pushed around by family members. He is very degrading to you if, he thinks you're more educated and financially stable because this makes him feel more like a man. He needs you to be weaker than he is to make himself appear strong.

5) **"Poor Man"** -These men have no financial responsibilities in life. They do not pay bills and are irresponsible in financial matters. This is a man who is looking for you to handle all the financial responsibilities. He prefers for you to pay the bills as he continues to spend money on impulse. Money usually "burns a hole in his pocket". This man will get a paycheck on Monday and broke by Wednesday. This is a huge red flag, especially if he did not pay any of his bills. I would recommend asking him to show you a copy of his credit report. I can tell you now, if you really want this type of man, buckle your seat belt. You're in for a long bumpy ride of taking care of him. You will never be financially stable with this man and poor house here I come.

6) **"Unemployed Man"** – When you find that a man is habitually unemployed that is a huge "RED" flag and maybe a sign of a lack of education or stability. This man shows a sense of immaturity because he does not want to consistently handle his financial obligations. These men may not necessary need to be a college graduate; however they at least need a High School diploma or GED. He may have a job and or a trade, which would be a good thing and maybe not a degree. There is nothing wrong with a blue collar worker, the key word being "worker". If, you meet a man who claims he's in between jobs, see if he's collecting unemployment, and is he still paying his own bills. Why? If he's really in between jobs and collecting unemployment, that means he at least is telling you the truth. He is capable of working a job. But be careful, all you need is six months of work history to collect unemployment. He could be one of those habitually unemployment check kind of guys. He works six months, then collects unemployment checks for twenty six weeks, then works six months, then collects unemployment checks and so on. You need to leave this man on the shelf and not take him down to play. This is another type of man that will never be financially stable enough to take care of himself much less a family.

7) **"The Baby Wipes Men"** - Do you really want that "living at home with his mama type of guy"? The man that cannot make a move without his momma's approval. Or that man that is happy living off his momma and has no real incentive to move out and become independent. Or, that man who's living off his parents for everything including all his finances.

You develop a relationship and you notice that his parents continue to pay his rent, buy his food, purchase him cars, etc... Now, you both are living together six months later and you can't understand why he won't get a real job and he's always asking his parents for money. Did you not see that great big old "Red Flag"? When you met and all during the time you were dating he was living off his parents and he's twenty five years old. Really, what did you think was going to change about this man? Then you find those men pushing late thirties early forties who's very comfortable being home with momma and not interested in leaving unless they find another momma, "you" to take care of them. They have no intention of growing up or being financially independent or yet responsible. It's a totally different story if the man has moved back to his parents to take care of them in their senior years, or while they're ill. Truthfully, you really want that type of man who has love and compassion for his parents. He will always have love and compassion for you and your family.

8) **"The Seed Man"** - These men like to fertilize the grass. They are fertilizers of the soil, all soil. They are not picky as to the location of the soil. They want to spread their sperm making baby after baby without a care in the world. You know what they say "momma's baby and daddy's maybe". They know they are getting women pregnant like a badge of honor or being a member of gang counting kills. They do not wear condoms and are high risk for spreading diseases. This man will tell you anything to get you to have sex with him without condoms. They are not interested in you or the child's welfare and have no inten-

tion of providing emotional or financial support. It's one thing to date men who have three or four children with an ex-wife, the key word being "X" wife who is financially stable and handling his responsibilities to those children. However, to date men who have three to four baby mommas, with every woman he stayed long enough to impregnate her and move on. Nevertheless, be careful, if you are going to date a man who has an "X" and children because that's less money for you and your family. Is he financially stable to support his previous family and you without you kicking in money to help him pay his child support and alimony? This is not a long term relationship kind of guy for your future, if he is not financially stable. I know, money does not matter. It's different because he loves you and not that other woman "Yeah, right". Be prepared to live in the poor house and help him pay bills the rest of your life.

9) **"The Milk Man"** When you see this type of man "RUN," and do not get on his milk delivery list. He's normally very, very good looking, attractive, and goes from house to house, or apartment complex leaving milk at the door. You know the type, when you were growing up how the milk man used to go around to the back porch and leave the glass containers of milk in the milk box. Then next week, he would come around and pick up the empties and leave more milk. This type of man is always looking to expand his route. He wants to bed as many women as possible, but he's lazy. He wants them all close by, so he does not have to put himself out with traveling expenses. As long as he's going in the back

door, none of the other women can see him. This man will always come to your house late in the dead of night; stay a couple of hours or come early, early in the morning just in time for you to sleep with him, get up and fix him breakfast. Then he will leave just before you and all the other women have to go to work. He never takes you out anywhere. He does not spend any money and will always ask you if you have any money to pay for the food. This man will probably always want to wear a condom which is good, "limits the risk of diseases," because he's really not interested in getting every woman pregnant in the neighborhood or a wholesome relationship. The key word is "limited". I did not say no risk of diseases because of course you know nothing is 100% effective.

10) **"The Drug Dependent Man"** -When you meet his man how do I say "run to the nearest exit, don't walk". This man is never going to be good for you and may introduce you into a world of drugs you really don't want to experience. Women, stop, look, and listen" because you cannot save these men. Really, *stop* and take the time to *look* at these men's habits, *listen* to their conversations. Have they smoked, drink, or use any type of drugs in their past. Why do you think you can change him, or he will change for you? Most likely you will be the one changing for him? If you don't like cigarette smoke and that man smokes, don't date him. He's not going to stop smoking. He's going to tell you when you meet him he was smoking. Why should I stop? The same thing with weed. He is not going to stop smoking weed. I met a young lady who was telling me a story about

her sister. She shared how her sister's boyfriend smoked weed. Her sister never smoke when they met, because of their childhood. They were always very upset because from a very young age their mother use cocaine. Both of them hated the fact that their mother used this drug, but the mom was always able to maintain a job and take care of them. Finally, the sister came to her and let her know she was hooked on crack cocaine. To her this was worse than the mom snorting cocaine. The sister was telling her she needed help. Everything in her house was gone. They had sold everything including the television to buy drugs. She had even committed fraud to get money to support the habit of her and her man. When she met this man, he was only smoking weed. One day he got her to try weed and they began smoking together. He then started lacing the joints with crack cocaine. She never knew this until she was hooked on the crack. Then of course they both started hitting the crack pipe. I believe that he already used crack at one time or another and wanted his woman in the same boat with him. Why? It's much easier to row that boat with two people. If he gets tire of rowing he can make her row. This is the problem: Both young ladies come from a mother with substance abuse and addictive behaviors. If you know that you have that in your upbringing stay away from these men. You may not be strong enough to resist the same weakness you hated in your mother. What I really don't understand is how she was sooooo…..upset, she could not believe how her sister could get hooked on crack cocaine. I'm surprise because this same sister smokes weed herself with her man. She claimed she smoked it before, but never on a regular until she started dating her current man. She continued to confess she would never smoke crack cocaine, weed was okay and it's not like a real drug. I tried to convince her to rethink her situation. I explained how her sister did not wake up one day and say, "I want to smoke crack cocaine." Like with anything else, it was a progression toward that drug with her man pushing. How do you know, your man will not lace your joint with crack cocaine? Why, because you think he loves you so much? It's sad, both women had self-image issues and addictive personalities which stem from their mom's addictive behavior. Remember what we talked about "Generation to generation dependency".

FYI: As women we need to learn what our own personality traits are and your standard level. When women settle for the same man with the above **ten personality traits**, the man is not the problem, it's the woman. It's your level of expectation, is your self-worth, and self-image so low that you are not looking for a good man with character before you get too involved with him. Do you have a clear understand of your own dating expectations? Do you have unresolved commitment issues being carried into the relationship? Be really realistic and ask yourself the hard questions. Do you really want to be another baby momma? *Financial instability*: Do you want to live in poverty and difficulty with financial hardships the rest of your life? *Cheater*: Do I really want to be the other woman sharing a man? *Married Man*: Do I want to always be a bridesmaid and never a bride? *Abuser*: Do you really want to be with someone kicking your Bundt cake (mentally or physically) every day?

Dare to Say NO: When asked to identify THE single thing that most contributed to his success in business, billionaire Warren Buffet's responded that it was his ability to "say no to 99 out of every 100 opportunities" that came his way. If an opportunity doesn't serve your current priorities, it isn't for you! Learning how to say "no" to the wrong things opens the door for the right opportunities to present themselves. It might not make you popular, but it will set you free.

Don't let your life be a mere reaction to what happens in everyone else's. Let focus put you back in the driver's seat. You have to know when to say "no." It doesn't necessarily make you a hero to put other's needs above your own. Too often, it just breaks your focus. Source: *"The only reason men fail is broken focus" (Mike Murdock)." By Coach Felicia.* This was re-stated so well by Coach Felicia, I don't think I could have put it better myself. You may have to say no to 99 men out of 100.

When that right one comes along you will really know it. He will serve your current priorities and focus in life. He will be your true soul mate to enhance you and bring your life to the next level of happiness and wealth. Remember this if you do not remember anything else *"think of men as pieces of clothing to be packed in a set of luggage".* You're getting ready to go on a trip and you must pack your suitcase, so you pack all you want, everything you know you can't do without.

That suitcase is so full, you have to sit your butt on it to get it closed. Then all of a sudden, this man comes along and says to you "baby can you open your suitcase and pack a few of my items." You think about this and you know that if you pack a few of his items, then some of yours must go. The suitcase can only hold but so much. So you're thinking and thinking….. You know you need your clothes, hair products, tooth paste, tooth brush, and so on.

You know you have absolutely no room at all. What do you do? If you are going to toss some of your most important items out of your suitcase to accommodate this man, you better make sure he's worth it, or why bother. You're a child of God and he will there in your corner. All you need to do is ask, believe and receive.

Seven Types of Women Men Should Avoid Dating in 2011

Married and taken-Guys if the woman you come across has a boyfriend or husband, leave her alone. Sometimes these women are ill-equipped to communicate with the men in their lives, when problems arise. It's a matter of respect when it comes to another man's wife or girlfriend. If you're being approached by that kind of woman send her home to her husband or boyfriend, she's not worth your time. You can do better than to get up with someone who is taken. They have nothing to offer you anyway.

Hood rats and felons-This is a growing problem with men today. They will disregard women who are intelligent, classy, educated, and have their stuff together for a loud, not so intelligent, obnoxious and ratchet women. If you had a good woman dating or married, why would you trade down?

Hood rats are only going to bring you down. They're probably not the kind of women you want to be bringing to meet your family and friends. Dismissing women who not potential mates.

High maintenance and Overly-flirty Divas-This type of woman can be the most aggravating to deal with because she's constantly surrounded by men. She needs a balance in her friends meaning she's got an equal number of male and female friends. You want someone who's not constantly craving attention from the male audience. A woman may not have that many male friends. If she has more male than female friends that maybe a red flag. It could be a sign that she's an excessive flirt. Women who are too high maintenance are often insecure and stuck on themselves. Deal with women who are level headed and down to earth.

Emotionally and psychologically weak- Women who don't have it in them to handle their own can be a challenge an example, is a women who allows another man to interfere in their relationship. A woman who is confident will be able to handle a man that is secure.

Financially irresponsible-This is another one to watch out for. You don't want to deal with someone who is "fiscally irresponsible". If she does not pay her bills on time or able to manage a savings or checking she is more than likely financially irresponsible. She's buying things she does not need or she often buys on impulse this is a sign of financial irresponsibility.
If she is maxing out her credit cards, this too is a sign. Huge red flag is a woman with bad credit and lawsuits because she owes people money.

Lacking employment and educational standards- Chronic unemployment could be a sign of immaturity. A mature women will have some kind of gainful employment or and educational goals. A woman who is mature will have a plan in place for her future. This plan has a timeline.

Living at home with parent(s) - It's okay to live at home if you're caring for your elderly or sick parent(s), in school, or you are dealing with a physical, psychological, or emotional challenge. However, if you're past the age of twenty five and you're still living at home with your parent(s), this could be an issue. There could be no real incentive to move out on your own. Perhaps the parents are enablers. This woman is looking for a man to be daddy to replace the parents...

In meeting women always check out her character and personality. If you meet a good woman who has her head on straight, don't let her go. Good women don't come along often. A real man desires someone who will make a good partner. They want someone they can bring around their family and friends. Keep this in mind though; if your family and friends are hinting to you that the woman you are dating is not someone suited for you, pay close attention. You would be surprised how the people around you can see things that you can't see. Part of dating is to seek out the best and not settle for less. If you leave a good women and trade down, reevaluate yourself. Is it possible that there is something in you that feels it's not worthy of the best. Evaluate the kind of women you attract. If you attract trifling, ratchet, immature, needy women, there's something about you that attracts those types. If you have a good woman who treats you good and respects you, that's a blessing.

Bottom line, do not allow anyone to come between you and your relationship.

Chapter 9 – Lust vs. Love

Men don't always want what is easy. They are hunters and like a challenge, even after they are married. Notice when you don't have relations for a while, he becomes, nice, sweet, and attentive. Your man will cater and be aware of your every need. Your name turns into, Baby and Sweetheart. Sugga, pats you on your bottom, rub your back.

When he's right where you want him, ask him to do something for you he would not normally do. Perhaps, have him to run to the store to get you something, anything you can think of, but make the task a little bit difficult. Blow in his ear, touch him a little bit. In a low sweet voice tell him, "to be quick because you are waiting."

So of course, he's running to the store to get you a candy bar and a coke. When he returns, you reward your man with hours and hours of love making. Then right after you finish giving him all of your essence. Ask him for a drink of water from the kitchen *(which is probably less than 20 feet from the bedroom)* or anything to make him get out of the bed to do something for you. Will he do it or tell you to get your own drink of water?

Is your relationship Lust or Love? Love will make him get up and get you that drink of water. Lust will tell you to get your own and while you're in there get him one too. **Reason**: Now that he have been satisfied he goes back to the beginning of the cycle.

He's moody and has a lot less passion. He's no longer calling you sweet names or patting you on your butt. You do not know why. So you decide to go take a shower to put him back on track. You are butt naked in the shower. He comes into the bathroom, gets in the shower, and ask you to pass the soap. My man, washes up, rinses off, and gets out. **Are you kidding me?**

He does not look at you and will not say one word other than, "hand me a towel." What wrong, why is he treating me like this? Believe me Sister, when you are in the shower butt naked, all soaped up, and he simply gets in the shower, turns his back, ask you to pass the soap, wash, and get out, he's not that into you.

You are a jump off chick or simply a "booty call". You are not that "put a ring on it type of girl".

You really need to be listening to Beyoncé, when she says "to the left". Even if you are both tired and you cannot have sex again, he should still be attentive to you.

Sister Girl, if he's getting into the shower you should be washing him. He should be washing you accompanied with sensual touching. Not, pass the soap and get out! **Are you kidding me?** Love is about more than just sexual intercourse.

Women need to learn, not just know the difference between the two, yes they both start with the letter "L" but they are spelled differently and they have two distinct different meanings.

LOVE = **Love** is an emotion of a strong deep affection and personal attachment. Love is also said to be a virtue representing all of human kindness, compassion, and affection — "the unselfish loyal and benevolent concern for the good of another". Love may describe compassionate and affectionate actions towards other humans, one's self or animals.

LUST = **Lust** is an emotion or feeling of intense desire in the body. The lust can take any form such as the lust for knowledge, the lust for sex or the lust for power. Lust is a powerful psychological force producing intense wanting for an object, or circumstance fulfilling the emotion. Many religions **separate the definition** of passion and lust by further categorizing lust as type of passion for something that does not belong to oneself.

Now, I am not saying that if you are married or you're in a long term monogamy relationship that your man will not get moody from time to time. There are days they just don't want to be bothered. It does not mean he has fell out of love with you and you're at the lust stage. You, being women can really dig down deep into your soul and you can tell if your man has really lost his interest.

Monogamy: *(the practice of being married or having a sexual relationship with only one partner during a period of time).* Then there is **Zoology** *(the practice of having only one mate at a time or during a lifetime).*

Ephesians 6:10-13 *finally, brethren, be strengthened in the Lord and in the might of his power. Put you on the amour of God that you may be able to stand against the deceits of the devil. For our wrestling is not against flesh and blood; but against principalities and powers,* *against the rulers of the world of this darkness, against the spirits of wickedness in the high places. Therefore, take unto you the amour of God that you may be able to resist in the evil day and to stand in all things perfect.*

FOUR REASONS WOMEN CHEAT

Many women who cheat are reacting to relationship problems or low self-image. Find out four common reasons why women cheat on their partners.

Relationship problems may trigger infidelity and explain why women cheat. The reasons may include:

> **To get out of a bad relationship.** Women who cheat may want to escape their relationship, and not know how to do it. Sometimes it's too hard to say you want out, so women cheat instead. Infidelity "is a way of sabotaging the relationship because for whatever reason the woman is already unhappy, dissatisfied, disgruntled, and wants out," says Ruggera.

> **To find that spark.** With money worries, exhaustion, bills, and kids, the spark that kept a relationship hot at first can often fizzle out. "Romance can get lost in the day-to-day routine of life," says Ruggera. Even if they're not on the hunt for an affair, some women may become seduced by the temptation of the "high" that comes with any new relationship.

> **An unsatisfying sex life.** If the sex isn't satisfying and a woman isn't feeling emotionally fulfilled in her relationship, "her interest may wander toward other men," says Ruggera. A woman can also start to feel

like she's unattractive or her partner doesn't desire her if their sex life is slow.

➢ **Revenge and retaliation.** If a husband has cheated, sometimes a woman may cheat to get back at him. It's an effort to get the husband to feel "the hurt, anger, and jealousy that she felt," says Ruggera.

Women Who Cheat: Problems Within

➢ **Low self-image** can be another reason why women cheat. "Gaining attention from men can boost their self-confidence and self-image," says Ruggera. "Compliments, phone calls, flowers, and notes from another man are flattering and make a woman feel more attractive and wanted."

➢ Another reason why **women** — and men — cheat is that they do what they know. If they saw infidelity in their parents' relationship, both men and women may follow those patterns in their own lives.

Women vs. Men

➢ Women who cheat do so for many of the same reasons that men do — attraction issues, unsatisfying sex life, unhappy relationship, feelings of neglect, looking for an ego boost, and a disconnect in the marriage.

➢ "Women are not that different from men when it comes to cheating, except that they are more apt to fall in love with their new partner," says Ruggera. The reason is hormonal — oxytocin, a hormone, stimulates the brain to give a woman that rush from being in love.

➢ Perhaps because of that, women are also more likely to care about the emotional aspects of infidelity when their partners cheat. In a recent study published in the journal *Personality and Individual Differences*, female victims of cheating asked about sex in just 29 percent of cases but about love in 71 percent of cases, compared with 57 percent and 43 percent of cases, respectively, for men.

Working on Intimacy

➢ If you want to protect your relationship from the temptation (and destruction) of infidelity, know that it needs to be nurtured and cared for — water it, feed it, give it love and sunlight to watch it grow and blossom.

➢ "The most effective way to keep a relationship or marriage healthy is to work on it every day and evaluate it on a regular basis," suggests Ruggera, adding that if a couple makes a concentrated effort to make a relationship a priority, enjoy time together, and work on communication, they can avoid feeling like they need someone else to make them happy. clear Article from: *Source:*

Chapter 10 –Hooking up/ jumping off

Some women hooking up and jump off is done for different reason than men. Some women may not be getting what they need in their relationship sexually. Some women hook-up and jump off because they are in a stage where they want no commitments. Yes, some women like men do experience commitment phobia. I know it may be hard to believe but some women, just like men, have no emotional attachment to their lover. They hook up because they need to be physically satisfied.

I talked to women who have admitted to several encounters with men where they just hooked up and jumped off. I could have written about other women under this section of the book, but this man's story was the one that really peak my interest. It peak my interest because I was so surprised by this person's encounters. Number one, she had previously touted how happily married she was. This was her first marriage and was not planning on divorcing.

Why are some men prone to sexual promiscuity? Vs. Why are some women prone to sexual promiscuity? This includes hooking up with partners of non-sexual attractions.

Case Study #7 – **Jane' Story**

My Sister girl, told me that she began hooking up with various service men that would come to her home. First, it was the plumber, then the air condition man, and finally the carpenter. Girl admitted, challenges with her weight and the fact that due to medical issues her husband was no longer meeting her sexual needs. Despite the love she and her husband shared for one another, their sex life was declining. First she tried personal stimulation to satisfy her cookie, but it was not enough.

One day a repairman who came to her house made a pass at her. This lingered on her mind for days, taunting her. When she knew her husband wasn't going to be home for hours, she broke a faucet knowing the plumber who had previously flirted with her perhaps would come and fix her plumbing. No pun intended.

These encounter continued twice a month for about six months. Then she began her air conditions adventure. . For some reason, these hook-ups got easier for her each time. She really didn't think twice about the air condition man. This encounter was over two months. She continued this behavior and found herself looking for the next rolling pin.

My girl did not understand or realize how these encounters would change her personally. My question to her would be "why would she be shocked because these encounters were so impersonal"? **Are you kidding me?** Why would she think she would get personal emotional commitment from any of these hook-ups? My girl was leaving her essence behind with each and every encounter and didn't know it!

Her last encounter was with the carpenter. The next day, she felt exhausted when her husband asked her if she was coming down with the flu or something because she slept so long. My question would be, have you been tested for HIV and sexually transmitted diseases. I know my girl always told me she was making sure they used rolling pin covers, but you never know.

Topic: Casual Sex Can Lead to Long-Term Relationships

People who "hook up" for casual sex can have as rewarding long-term relationships as those who take it slowly and establish a meaningful connection before they have **sex**, says a new study. University of Iowa researchers analyzed relationship surveys and found that average relationship quality was higher for people who took it slowly than for those who became sexually involved in "hook-ups," casual dating, or "friends with benefits" relationships.

However, having sex early on wasn't the reason for this disparity, according to UI sociologist Anthony Paik. He factored out people who weren't interested in getting serious and he found that those who became sexually involved as friends or acquaintances and were open to a serious relationship were just as happy as those who dated but **delayed having sex**. The study analyzed a survey of 642 heterosexual adults in Chicago. To measure the quality of the relationships, people answered questions about how much they loved their partner, their level of satisfaction with intimacy in the relationship, the future of the relationship, and how their lives would be different if the relationship ended.

"We didn't see much evidence that relationships were lower quality because they started off as hook-ups," Paik, an assistant professor in the College of Liberal Arts and Sciences, said in a UI news release. "The study suggests that

97

rewarding relationships are possible for those who delay sex. But it's also possible for true love to emerge if things start off with a more 'Sex and the City' approach, when people spot each other across the room, become sexually involved and then build a relationship," he added. *Source: The study is published in the August issue of the journal Social Science Research. Last Updated: 09/01/2010*

Love It and Kick It!

Maybe we need to go back to the drawing board on this one. 642 heterosexuals adults in Chicago seem like that's a mere fraction of the population. In my fifty nine years of experience with all of the women and men that I have encounter over the years speak more toward delaying sexual relationship. Of, course the men seemed to be more interested in having sex sooner rather than later as opposed to the women. Some women who yielded to temptation regretted it.

My sisters, rise above it. If you should befall weakness, all is not lost because GOD is a forgiving GOD.

1 Corinthians 10:13 *Let no temptation take hold on you, but such as is human. And God is faithful, who will not suffer you to be tempted above that which you are able: but will make also with temptation issue, that you may be able to bear it.*

One must learn from one mistake to grow and move on in life and not dwell in the past. Like my mother use to say, "There is nothing you can do about spilled milk." However, once you spill milk out of the bottle, all you can do is wipe up.

I have always been a believer that each sexual encounter will take a part your of soul. Once gone, you are unable to recover that missing piece. Some way you must be able to rise above it, forgive yourself, and move on. Men have the side of their brain that allows them to detach the physical from the emotional it allows them to move on quicker than women.

INTERNET'S DIRTY SECRET: ASSESSING THE IMPACT OF ONLINE INTERMEDIARIES ON THE OUTBREAK OF SEXUALLY TRANSMITTED DISEASES

New York University - Leonard N. Stern School of Business <u>*Anindya Ghose*</u> *New York University - Leonard N. Stern School of Business April 6, 2012*
Abstract: *We investigate how the expansion of Craigslist into different states over a 11 year period in the United States affected the incidence of HIV. Using a natural experiment setup, we identify the effects of Craigslist's entry on HIV trends by exploiting the variations across states and time. After controlling for extraneous factors, our results show that Craigslist's entry leads to a 19.8 percent increase in HIV cases, which maps out to an average of 158.7 cases for a state in a year. The analyses further suggest that non-market related casual sex serves as the underlying mechanism driving the increase in HIV cases, while paid transactions (e.g., escort services and prostitution) solicited on the site do not influence HIV trends. The increases in HIV cases as a result of Craigslist entry are estimated to impose treatment costs of over $118 million annually on the U.S. healthcare system. Study implications and limitations are discussed.*
File Name: SSRN-id2150282.; © *2013 Social Science Electronic Publishing*

Chapter 11 –Secrets & Infidelity, What is it?

TOPIC: 'SEXTING' COMMON FOR THOSE WHO CHEAT: STUDY. RESEARCH FINDS THESE ONLINE EXCHANGES ARE NOW PART OF EXTRA-MARITAL MATING.

FRIDAY, June 24 (Health Day News) — A new study finds that the practice of "sexting" — sending salacious texts or nude photos over the Internet — is now a key tool for Americans bent on infidelity.

Sexting, which notoriously cost former Democratic Congressman Anthony Weiner his job, is "alive and well," said sociologist Diane Kholos Wysocki, the study's lead author. In fact, she said, it's a part of the whole extra-marital mating ritual, according to Wysocki, who said adulterous interactions that begin online seem to follow a regular pattern.

"People meet, then they send pictures, then they send naked pictures, then they proceed and ultimately meet if they find that they're compatible," she said.

The study, based on a survey of almost 5,200 users of a website devoted to extra-marital dating called ashleymadison.com, doesn't say anything about the habits of the American population in general. And, as Kholos Wysocki acknowledged, its value is also limited because it only includes those people who volunteered to take part and were already using the site. "Any time you get a group of people on the Internet, we can't say its representative," said Kholos Wysocki, a professor of sociology, University of Nebraska at Kearney.

However, she said the survey does offer insight into why people choose to stay married but still have **affairs**. As of a year ago, the ashleymadison.com site, whose motto is "Life is short. Have an affair," claimed more than 6 million members. Working with the site, Kholos Wysocki in 2009 posted a survey for members with 68 questions. The results appear in a recent online issue of the journal *Sexuality& Culture*. Those who responded tend to be upscale (with a median income of about $86,000), mostly married (64 percent) and highly educated (about 70 percent attended college, and 20 percent had advanced degrees). More than 6 out of every 10 respondents were male.

Sixty percent of the women and close to half of the men said they'd engaged in sexting -- sending naked photos of themselves via email or cell phone. Age was no bar for the practice, since about 40 percent of people over the age of 50 had done so. However, sexting was much more likely among the few surveyed who were aged 19-24.

About three-quarters of people of both genders acknowledged having cheated while in a serious **relationship**. More than 8 in 10 women and two-thirds of men said they'd met people in person after first encountering them online. That suggests many users plan on consummating an extra-marital relationship, not just looking and flirting online.

Jeffrey T. Parsons, professor of psychology at Hunter College in New York City, said, "The finding isn't surprising. People who are going to use a website to look for extramarital affairs are probably willing to go the distance, as it were," he said. "Sure, there are probably some who just use the website for the titillation factor and the sense of thrill and danger and perhaps "being bad." But the nature of the website no doubt attracts those who are interested in **more than just cybersex**."

In some cases, spouses weren't kept in the dark. "There were a number of them who went on there with their spouses, looking to add to their sex life," Kholos Wysocki noted. Psychology professor Parsons explained that "there are adults in consensual relationships in which sexting, cybersex, and even in-person **sexual relations** with other people are negotiated and allowed."

What has the Internet's overall impact been on adultery? "You can't blame cheating on the Internet," Kholos Wysocki reasoned. "People who don't have the Internet are still cheating." However, she said, the Internet has probably made it easier to find new partners. "It takes less time," she said. Last Updated: 06/24/2011. By Randy Dotinga, Health Day News.

Is Casual Sex Good for You?

New research shows that it is possible for both men and women to enjoy sex with no strings attached.

Some people think that men can enjoy casual sex without getting attached, while women tend to be more at risk of "catching" feelings and experiencing emotional turmoil as a result of loveless **hookups**.

However, a new study seems to disprove that theory, and instead, it appears that sex can be mutually beneficial regardless of whether you are a man or a woman and regardless of whether you are having a hookup or you are having sex with a longtime partner. In other words, the study (which was published in *The Journal of Sex Research*) found that the benefits associated with sex appear to be the same whether you are in a relationship or simply enjoying casual sex.

The researchers surveyed almost 400 people in their mid-twenties and found that women reported feeling physically satisfied nearly 93 percent of the time, while 78 percent reported feeling a thrill or a rush. Almost 67 percent of women said that having sex helped cheer them up when they had a bad day.

Notably, the study did show that women felt more guilt and apprehension when they enjoyed casual sex **without using protection**. (They also found that women were more likely to practice safer sex when they had sex with a friend as opposed to a "traditional" hookup.) In other words, friends-with-benefits might be beneficial indeed, at least for sexual health.

However, it is worth noting that this is just one study. Many women struggle to reach orgasm (only 30 percent reach it through intercourse alone), so these statistics seem a little high. Reaching orgasm 93 percent of the time is wonderful, but it could also be unrealistic: Even women in long-term and passionate relationships often have trouble **reaching orgasm** each and every time. Having sex with someone who doesn't know you and your specific hot spots can only lead to more sexual difficulty as every woman's interests and desires are different.

Still, the study does show that the sexual climate in our country is changing, particularly among young people. Women feel more empowered to enjoy sex and to express their sexual desires, and that's a healthy and significant step in the right direction. But it's important to note that casual sex isn't for everyone and not everyone (man or woman) will be able to enjoy intimacy without becoming emotionally attached. Additionally, for some people, it can be harder to express their likes and dislikes to someone they don't know as opposed to someone they love and trust.

Casual sex also comes with risks attached, which is why it is so important to **always practice safe sex** and to get tested for sexually transmitted infections or diseases regularly. It's also crucial to use wisdom when hooking up or having one-night stands — you don't really know that guy at the bar, no matter how cute or "normal" he might seem, and going home with a complete stranger is always dangerous. Practice safety and good self-care, and you will be able to enjoy sexual pleasure as well as sexual and physical health.

Last Updated: 01/11/2013
By **Laura Berman, PhD**

Definitions for Infidelity(noun)want of faith or belief in some religious system especially a want of faith in or disbelief of the inspiration of the Scriptures of the divine origin of Christianity Infidelity(noun)unfaithfulness to the marriage vow or contract violation of the marriage covenant by adultery Infidelity(noun)breach of trust unfaithfulness to a charge or to moral obligation treachery deceit as the infidelity of a servant, **lack of belief in a religion; a: unfaithfulness to a moral obligation : DISLOYALTY B: marital unfaithfulness or an instance of it**

What's the definition of infidelity? The best definition I can come up with is any act committed by a person who is in a committed relationship that violates the circle of trust and love. Infidelity is complex because it is not black and white. Would you consider your partner frequently keeping in touch with their ex as a sign of infidelity? Would you consider your husband confiding in a female friend as a sign of cheating? Would you consider your girlfriend chatting with a new friend she met online as a sign of betrayal? Infidelity starts with a lie, then a lie to cover the original lie and then a series of lies to cover shameless acts of betrayal.

People often confuse between emotionally attaching themselves and a platonic friendship. When you are in a platonic friendship you don't think about your friend often. When you are emotionally involved you think of them more often

106

than you should and sometimes more often than your spouse or partner. You may not think you are cheating, but the fact is you are cheating. This is called emotional infidelity.

Emotional infidelity often leads to infidelity in its ugliest form tearing apart from relationships, creating deep wounds in hearts and wrecking families and their loved ones.

Time to Act: Now is the time for you to act. Whether you want to confirm your fears or catch your partner or spouse cheating on you with evidence, I can help you.

CAN A MARRIAGE SURVIVE INFIDELITY?

Infidelity is a threat to marriage, but it's not always an insurmountable issue. Learn how to repair a marriage after one spouse is unfaithful.

When former California governor (and movie star) Arnold Schwarzenegger and his wife, journalist Maria Shriver, recently announced they were separating, everyone speculated as to why the celebrity couple would call it quits after 25 years of marriage. Two weeks later, the truth came out: Schwarzenegger fathered a child with a woman who worked in their home. Shriver moved out of their mansion shortly after her husband confessed about the affair, which took place over a decade ago.

Schwarzenegger's public admission of his affair and love child brings cheating back into the headlines, but marital infidelity is nothing new. Reliable statistics on the subject are hard to find, but some estimates suggest that 25 percent of husbands and 15 percent of wives have been unfaithful — and even more have thought about it.

When infidelity occurs, it can obviously cause a deep rift in the relationship between a husband and wife. And when the cheating involves major secrets, like hidden children, it can destroy a marriage permanently. But the reality is that many unfaithful marriages can be salvaged, says Tina B. Tessina, PhD, a psychotherapist and author of *Money, Sex and Kids: Stop Fighting about the Three Things That Can Ruin Your Marriage*. "As a therapist who works with couples every day, I can categorically state that it is possible to repair the marriage after infidelity," says Dr. Tessina.

The problem with infidelity is that we are programmed to believe that it is the gravest of all marital offenses. In reality, problems such as alcoholism, overspending, and verbal and **emotional abuse** can be just as bad. "I strongly disagree with the attitude most of the press seems to have that infidelity is such a trauma," she says. "Sometimes it is, but often the person who has been cheated on has contributed to the problem."

Surviving Infidelity

Of course, causes of marital infidelity vary widely from couple to couple. As a result, the answer to whether a marriage can be saved after infidelity must be determined on a case-by-case basis. "It really depends on why they were unfaithful and what the history is with the spouse," says Leslie Seppinni, PsyD, a psychologist in private practice in Beverly Hills, Calif. "If the spouse is unfaithful because the relationship is falling apart or because they feel **lonely** or neglected, then usually there is a decision to make on whether to stay together or not. If it's something like a long-term affair or multiple affairs, then you have some real soul-searching to do because there are major trust issues, and whether or not you can overcome those issues is the key."

Regardless of the severity of the infidelity, you both must be committed to the reconciliation or it won't work, says Steven M. Sultanoff, PhD, a professor of psychology at Pepperdine University in Malibu, Calif. "If the answer to the question, 'What do I truly want?' is to remain in the **relationship**, then it is worth salvaging," he says. "Both of you must be committed to healing the relationship — you to forgive and your spouse to explore and examine his or her motivation for being unfaithful."

What Can Help After Marital Infidelity

If you decide to give your relationship another try, you're likely to need the help of a counselor to work through your issues successfully, says Tessina. The process starts with reopening the lines of communication. "If you're serious about fixing the problems in your relationship, it's crucial that you both begin to face each other honestly and openly," she says. "It's time to take an honest look at what went wrong."

Next, you need to make an active effort to fix the problems that confront your relationship. Here again, a counselor may be needed to help with the process. Finally, you need to be able to forgive one another before you can move on with your lives together. "Forgiving each other doesn't mean condoning what happened — that would mean it would be okay if it happened again," says Tessina. "What it does mean is that you're willing to close that chapter and move on."

When it's Time to Let Go

Of course, not every relationship can — or should — be salvaged. And if you feel like irreparable damage has been done, then it might be better for both of you to move on with your lives. Some of that decision can be based on the progress of your therapy, explains Tessina. "If your spouse changes his behavior and sincerely works to do whatever the therapist recommends, it's probably working. If the spouse is blaming, denying, and making excuses, then it's probably not," she says. Another way to evaluate progress: "If your relationship improves, it's probably working. If things remain the same, it's probably not."

Sometimes, you may discover that the relationship flaw that has driven you apart just cannot be fixed. As hard as that may be, often that's a sign that it's time to move on. "You cannot ask someone to completely change who they are to be with you," says Dr. Seppinni. "If you are asking for character changes, it might be best to walk away. It is important to be honest with yourself about the relationship when deciding whether it's time to end it."

By Wyatt Myers, Medically reviewed by Lindsey Marcellin, MD, MPH **Copyright © 2013 Everyday Health Media, LLC** about EverydayHealth.com | About Everyday Health Media, LLC

Chapter 12 – Are Foreigners Better?

Case Study #8 ~ **Hanna's Story**

Are foreign men better at loving relationships than American men or are they just the same. I had a close friend that I knew for years. She was a single mom that also suffered spousal abuse by a prior husband. She was closed to men for a long time and tried to develop relationships that never came. Until one day, she met this man who was in this country from the Dominican Republic. She is tall, Swedish and from Kenya, pure white skin and golden blonde hair.

Seeing this woman with a dark hair Dominican Republican man may not be the norm. She fell in love with this foreign man from the Dominican Republic and of course he did not have citizenship papers to stay in America. Almost, every day I talked to her she stated he was great and this man met her every need emotionally and sexually. She could not believe it she hit the jackpot because he was much younger.

I advised her to be careful because some foreigners are simply seeking citizenship. The relationship appeared to be moving very quickly. She was very upset with me because she believed he loved her. She started a construction business with this foreigner who ran all of the workers at all of the job sites. They worked with builders and made lots of money and I mean up into the millions of dollars. For some reason, she called me out of the blue upset about this man of her life. She has added his name to the business and they got married, she was also having a baby.

There was something going on but she could not put her finger on it. She could feel something in the pit of her stomach, but she pushes it down and forgot about it. She had the baby and this man convince her to send to the Dominican Republic some of his relatives. She had gotten them visa's to come to America. All of a sudden the money flow was not the same. She could not figure out why! Some of the builders were not being paid. This Foreigner kept giving her excuses for the builders.

Suddenly, in the midst she found herself with a new baby, household, and taking care of this man. He took on more of the running of the business. What is done in the dark will normally come to the light, sometimes sooner rather than later. He started staying out and stop being as conscientious as he was emotionally and physically.

Eventually, he left her. After he was gone, while she was digging into the business paperwork, she discovered that her husband had sent over five hundred thousand dollars in money orders to the Dominican Republic to his parents. He also had taken the architectural plans she had drawn up to build her dream home and built that same home for his parents in the Dominican Republic. **Are you kidding me?**

In addition, he had transferred her Mercedes to his cousin who was here from the Dominican Republic on a visa. She was totally in the dark and unaware, they had earned millions of American dollars. Apparently, the taxes on the business were never paid to the department of labor, which created a "Red Flag". She found herself in a fight with the builders because they had paid her husband directly instead of through normal channels.

He had disappeared and she had to literally become a private investigator to find him. Finally, after extensive research she found that he had walked away from their family *(his own child)* to be with a woman from the Dominican Republic, who he was now living with. To add insult to injury he told her he never wanted anything to do with American women, other than to get his green card. **Wow, Are you kidding me?**

I really care for my girlfriend Hanna and still do to this day. However what she forgot to do was to protect herself. She should have listened to that gut feeling in the pit of her stomach. She knew something was off and did not listen to her own intuition.

What is it about a man's love that makes some women forget about protecting themselves? What makes women so gullible? At one time or another women, we have all been tricked. What are the signs and why can't we see those signs coming. Do men have the inside track to what woman really want?

Are we guilty of giving them that temporary emotional and physical stimulation to get what they want? Or were we so mislead as a children because we did not get all those special ingredients in the right portions to ensure a high self-image. Does our self-image and emotional needs shift at the beginning, during, and after the relationship? Women may have highs and lows when they fall in love. Therefore, her self-image is in danger of dwindling in the life cycle of a woman.

Do men have such a heighten sense, that they can see the *"mark"* a mile away? Men may have something we don't, *"clear eyes".* It's something to think about. Is it possible that this man had no intention of being with this woman the rest of his life, till death do they part as stated in the marriage vows?

"You need to get past the train tracks before that train gets here"

Unfortunately, life does not work like that because all women must make their own mistake in life. It a learning curve, some of us have a fast one and others, not so much. Are men, cleverer than women and will they always be a step ahead of us? Do they have the insight to turn it on and off when necessary to give them the advantage?

Was he with her because he wanted his citizenship in order to gain wealth in America? He did invest several years of his life into a marriage before he got it. Was she in love, and he was not? Was this man on a mission to get something from this woman? He was much younger and culturally they had nothing in common. The relationship was not on equal terms at all. He came to this country poor.
She taught him everything she knew about the construction business.

Currently, this woman is not in a relationship. She confesses that she is tired of getting hurt. The silver lining in the situation is the daughter she was blessed to have out of that union. Where do we find the balance as woman to get the love we need, and not sacrifice our self-worth?

Case Study #9 ~ **Ashanti's Story**

I met another American woman, Ashanti whose husband was from the Africa. He also, did not have his citizenship papers. However, he was not a new comer to America. He could not read or write very well when he came to this country. He also knew nothing about business.

She, being a business woman started setting up businesses, teaching him along the way. He could not get his citizenship due to delays in the application. One year it expired and they had to start over. Another year they did not tell immigration and nationalization that they moved and was forced to start over again.

It took ten years and finally within the same year of him getting his citizenship he left her for another woman from his homeland. Her husband had always been a hard worker but something has always been off about their marriage. She could feel it down in the pit of her stomach. She gave him a son and owned several commercial buildings.

She told me how she got sick and he had no compassion toward her at all. She was finally hospitalized. While she was in the hospital, she found out that her husband had refinanced the buildings and pulled out the cash. She had turned over the responsibility of the buildings to him. Why? He continued to claim their marriage was based on lies because she did not trust him to take care the financial

115

responsibility of the business. She wanted to prove that she trusted him and loved her husband.

She got sick and for some reason, they no longer were intimate for over a year. He no longer had interest and did not want to touch her in that manner. Her illness got worst and she had to stay in the hospital for a long period of time, without any visitation from her husband.

When she was finally released from the hospital, there were foreclosure notices posted on the door of their commercial buildings as well as their home. She had to find her son and together they broke into the house. Her husband had cleaned it out, including the bedding they slept on and moved.

They had a commercial business together for years. He stole all the equipment and materials and put everything into five storage compartments. This man had taken everything they owned including over $500,000.00 from the bank.

She shared how her fifteen year old son had to live on the street and was washing up and getting water from the gas station. She could not understand why her husband would leave his only son on the street to fend for himself.

She started investigating her own husband and when they were building their home several years prior. He was building a house with a woman that he currently lives with from his homeland. She also found out that this woman had several children that she really believes down in her heart belong to him. Her husband continued to tell her the children were not his kids. However, he could not leave this woman because she had small children.

This is the million dollar question: How does a man walk away from his own biological child and cannot walk away from children that he claim are not his children? He refused to pay his wife child support or alimony. He refused to let her know where their joint assets were located. She could not get any of her personal items.

This man packed up this house lock, stock, and barrel while she was in the hospital. She found out where this woman and her husband set up house. She claimed she would drive up to the house and sit outside and cry her eyes out. He filed for a divorce, rented a house for him as a pretense to the courts. The house he rented was empty while his wife and child were living in a foreclosed home with no lights, heat or water.

The funny thing was that he in fact never moved into that house. He just needed a home address to give to the courts. He did not want the courts to know he was living with this woman from his homeland. How can you care so little for a woman you claimed you loved for over ten years. Leave your homeless while you rented an empty house for the purpose of an address. **Are you kidding me?**

She finally had to leave that home and bounced around from hotel to hotel. For some reason this woman who was extremely intelligent could not get herself together. Her life was crumbling in front of her eyes.

Finally she went to court and the judge order him to give his wife and son the keys to the house and pay the rent every month. Of course, he never paid the rent. The poor woman who owned the house was in the middle of a night mare *"war of the roses"* true story. The landlord could not get Ashanti out of her *(landlord)* house and the husband was not paying the rent. The landlord had nothing to do with Ashanti's situation regarding her divorce.

I was very surprised, because she had total disregard for another sister, who was her landlord. She took the position that it was not her problem. The landlord could take her husband to court. Was this woman was so bitter that she was taking out her frustration on all the people around her? The sweetness of this woman was disappearing and she did not realize it at all.

She was hurt and distress at her husband but was not directing that disappointment toward him. He had started to come around, making advances toward her professing his love for her and not the other woman. She stated he was always trying to be intimate with her like it was in the beginning. She was confused! **Are you kidding me?** He was trying to kiss and rub on her again to show he loved her and not this other woman.

For some reason this woman could not see that train coming down those railroad tracks.

They were both in the middle of a war of the roses divorce. He knew he would have to give back fifty percent of all the assets he stole including the $500,000.00. Each time alimony and child support payments presented itself, he would make sure he was intimate with his wife. He'd always leave the house saying, "I can't pay you this time, and can you call the courts to give me a delay." She would. **Are you kidding me?**

The courts would always reset the calendar date and she would not see him until it was time to make a court appearance again. This behavior went on for months. Did he ever go back to his wife? Well you will have to wait for Are you kidding me, book 2. What do you think?

What do I think? Sister Girl, when you're in a fight for your life, as Muhammad Ali would say "protect yourself at all times"

Chapter 13 – Pimp, Boyfriend or Friends?

I was just watching Jerry Springer and the show was, "I'm Your Pimp, Not Your Boyfriend". How stupid, yes I said it stupid is this woman?

Case Study #10 **Annette's & John's Story!**

Annette was first introduce as being a friend to the mom's son, John. At that time he was in a serious, ten year relationship with his baby's mother, Joy. The mom really did not think anything of it, until it was later discovered that Annette continued to have a relationship with her son. For over six months Annette had been in a love triangle but continued to tell herself John was her soul mate. The red flag was there over and over again. However, Annette continued to see John.

Finally it came to a head when the baby's mom, Joy confronted Annette about her man. He lived in a common law situation with Joy and their children in their home for over ten years. For some reason Annette never knew her man was pretty much married to his children's mother and she was the other woman.

Her boyfriend continued to lie to her over and over again. Annette talked to her boyfriend's common law wife, the lies were laid out on the table. Guess what? Annette continued to see this man. **Are you kidding me?** Annette is now emotionally attached. I bet she didn't see that train coming!

What the mom does not understand is how you can continue to call yourself in a relationship with a person, never really meeting the family members. The mom found out later that Annette pressured John to meet her. So, John set up a fake step mother as his mom.

John never stayed overnight at Annette's house. He could only spend a couple of hours here and there due to his work. He stayed away from Annette for days at a time. Newsflash, he's sleeping somewhere and he can't never take you to where he lives? **Are you kidding me?**

Annette is the mistress, refuses to recognize it, but feels it in her soul. However, she continues to believe John's lies over and over again. Does Annette have a low self-image? Is she missing some of the magic formula with those special ingredients? Finally Annette meets the real mom. John tried to control the meeting, making attempts to get his mom to lie to Annette that he never lived with Joy. **Are you kidding me?**

Do you think if the mom were to tell, the woman the truth, she would listen? No! John turns to Annette, who is clearly second choice, because now Joy has left him, and professes his love. Annette appears to be really happy.

The mom has had experience with her son prior and have advised women to run! The train is coming! Annette starts interacting with the mom and family members now that Joy is gone. So, is Annette really first? No, because John continues to make every attempt to get Joy back. Annette is fighting with John while they continue to move forward. She moves into John's house. Ladies, be careful what you ask for, that grass may not be as green as it looks.

Now all of the signs are there, Annette is the other woman, but she continues to move forward to concur the #1 spot. It's like driving on those train tracks, hoping you get to the end without that train showing up to crush your car. You have no information about the train schedule or when or if the train will come. However, you continue to drive on those train tracks.

John starts having financial problems after he lost his job. He also falls in a deep depression since Joy left him. He needs Annette to help him financially with his bills at his home. Annette wants that number one spot, so she jumps at the chance to move into his home. Mind you, they are still fighting everyday like cats and dogs. Annette claims she knows John, because she sleeps with him and no one understands him like her, not even the mother. **Are you kidding me?** First big mistake!

Why is it that some women feel that they know all about their man? No one can tell them anything because they have the best slice of sweet potato pie in the world. Here is the hundred thousand dollar question. How can a female of a six month relationship know a man better than his own mother who has raised him to the age of twenty eight years? Women need to understand that sweet potato pies is the same, with the same ingredients and pie crust. Some women may add a twist from woman to woman by adding lemon or more cinnamon.

Remember, he may not always be your boyfriend, but he will always be that mother's son!

Some women have more tricks than others in the cookie jar. Some women have more experience and some women can move better than others. But the cookies are the same, make no mistake about it. It feels and taste different to the man, because the love is different toward that woman. Some intimacy sessions are better than others because of the "Lust" or "Love" involved in the performance.

Now, Annette's lease for her apartment is not up and she's going to ruin her credit by breaking her lease. Annette is putting her man needs before her own by not paying rent to move into John's house. She is over the moon, she is the chosen one. However, she continues to call John's mother to claim that the son is a liar, he's a liar, and he is the biggest liar I have ever seen. **Are you kidding me?**

They continue to fight every day the same way he fought with his x-baby mother Joy. The mom is trying to give solid advice to Annette woman to woman. The mom tells Annette that she needs to slow down and take care of herself in this situation. However, Annette is really not listening, and she wants this man. In the same breath she claims he's the worst sort of liar.

Woman to woman, the mom tells Annette the common denominator in this formula is John in this relationship between her and Joy. Throughout this period neither Joy nor Annette have listened to the mom's advice. All they want is this man, the same man that has lied to both of them over and over again. This same man that gave both Joy and

Annette a sexually transmitted disease. **Are you kidding me?** How can these women claim he loves them with this type of betrayal and infidelity?

Instead of this being about these women taking care of themselves, it has become a cat fight about who will get this man. **Are you kidding me?** Really, is he that much of a prize? Let's see, he cheats, he lies, he has given both woman sexually transmitted disease and he could not commit to a solo relationship if his life depended on it.

This is a full blown cat fight, literally destroying both women and they refuse to see that train coming down those railroad tracks.

It's amusing how a strong low self-image prevails and destroys good women. Annette has finally moved out of her apartment to this man's house only to find evidence that Joy really lived there. Joy's clothes are in the drawers, all over the house, female products everywhere. Annette continues to believe this man when he tells her Joy never lived in this house. He claims he just moved those items from the storage compartment.

One, if this stuff was in storage it's clear at one point they lived together. Two, how did Joy's things get into the storage compartment together with this man? Then she's fighting with this man because the man does not want to move Joy's things from the house. At the same time, this man is calling Joy, telling her how he loves her. He's blaming Joy for forcing him to move Annette into the house because she left him with all the bills.

Annette and this man get into this knock down drag out fight and he throws all Annette's belongings on the lawn in front of the neighbors. Annette cries to the mom about John being a liar. The mom tells her, "You never knew Joy lived there? Annette states to the mom, "You just told me by what you said." **ARE YOU KIDDING ME?**

Sister Girl, you moved into a house with another woman belonging everywhere and you want to believe that she never lived there? Annette got so upset that she rented a truck and moved all of her things out of the house. Annette now has an eviction on her door because she used her rent money to pay John's bills at his house. Number one rule Annette, "protect yourself at all times".

The mom try's to call Annette and it's clear by now that she is back with John. **Are you kidding me?** Is a low self-image that debilitating? How much disrespect do you endure before you leave? What is the hold? Why can't Annette walk away? Will Annette survive this relationship, proving the mom wrong? We will see!

Was he a boyfriend to Annette or was he pimping her out to get his bills paid? Or was he a friend with benefits? You decide!

Case Study # 11 ~ **Cynthia's Story!**

I met a young lady who we are going to call Cynthia, who told me a story about her sister. Her boyfriend smoked weed and her sister had never smoked when they met. She and her sister had issues with drugs because when they were very young their mother and father used cocaine. Both girls hated the fact that their parents used, even though they were functional addicts. The parents were always able to maintain a job and take care of them. They even consistently lived in a nice home with both of their parents.

One day the sister came to the other and informed her that she was hooked on crack cocaine, which to her was worst then the mom snorting cocaine up her nose. The sister was telling her she needed help that everything in her house was gone. They had sold everything including the television to buy drugs. She also confessed that she committed fraud to get money to support their habit. When she met this man he was only smoking weed and one day he got her to try it and they began smoking together.

Then he started to lace the joints with crack cocaine. She never knew this until she was hooked. Then of course they both started hitting the crack pipe. Now, I believe that he already used crack at one time or another and wanted his woman in the same boat. Why? It's much easier to row that boat with two people and if he gets tired of rowing he can make her row.

BEING PIMPED OUT – YES OR NO!

Are either one or both of these women being pimped out to ensure the man has help rowing the boat? Why? Typically when someone gets hooked on any drug, they will do whatever is necessary to get that drug. Men know women are sitting on assets that can buy those drugs. Image this man thinking, "If she get hook, she's going to take care of

127

both of our drug needs" So again, pimp or boyfriend? **Are you kidding me?**

Both young ladies came from a mother with substance abuse and addictive behaviors. If you know that you have that in your DNA you may not be strong enough to resist the same weakness you hated in your mother while you were growing up.

Now, what I really don't understand is how she was sooooo.....upset, she could not believe how her sister could get hooked on crack cocaine. I'm surprise because this same sister smokes weed herself with her man. She claimed she smoked it before, but never on a regular until she started dating her current man.

She continued to assert how she would never smoke crack cocaine, weed is okay. It's not like a real drug. **Are you kidding me?** You may want to re-think that situation. Your sister did not wake up one day and say, "I want to smoke crack cocaine."

This situation holds like anything else, it was a progression toward that drug with her man pushing. How do you know, your man will not lace your joint with crack cocaine. Why because you think he loves you so much? It sad, but both women has self-image issues and addictive personalities which stem from their parents behaviors. Remember what we talked about "Generation to generation dependency".

FRIENDS WITH BENEFITS!

Do you have friend relationships with benefits and can you really handle that type of relationship?

What is the Definition of friends with benefits?

Two friends who have a sexual relationship without being emotionally involved. Typically two good friends who have casual sex without a monogamous relationship or any kind of commitment.

If you have some of those ingredients from chapter one missing in your formula as a woman you can't handle this type of relationship. If you're not made of strong stock with high self-image you will not survive the types of relationships listed below under the 10 Rules. Tread lightly!

10 Rules of Being Friends with Benefits

Rule 1: DO think twice about hooking up with your neighbor.

There are, without a doubt, many pros to having a FWB living in close proximity.

Rule 2: DON'T convince yourself the relationship is more serious than it is.
"No matter how hard sex buds try not to fall in love, there is always the possibility that one or both parties will catch feelings," says Russo. "And contrary to popular belief, it isn't just the ladies at risk of falling and ruining the no-strings-attached arrangement." It happens to men too. But "if you've been sleeping with a guy who confesses that he considers you nothing more than a sex bud, while you dream

of making him your boyfriend, it is best to cut ties and maintain a strict no-contact policy," urges Russo. "Don't think you'll change his mind. Just appreciate what you had and move on to the next."

Rule 3: DO proceed with caution if you meet someone new.
You don't need to hit the brakes immediately with your FWB when you meet someone new, says Amy Spencer, author of *Meeting Your Half-Orange: a Guide to Using Dating Optimism to Help You Meet Your Other Half*. "Don't assume exclusivity with a person you like until you've actually talked about it," she says. "Remember, you're not the only one having casual sex on the side while you date—maybe your new catch is too." The bottom line here: Don't make any major decisions until you've clarified things with your new dude.

Rule 4: DON'T encourage friends and family to hang out with your FWB.
Your FWB should fill the same role as an imaginary friend, says Spencer. He's there when you need him, but he has no place in your regular social life. Why? Well, first, because a FWB is meant to be temporary. If you start bringing him into your daily routine, you're creating a long-term connection. And second, because you have to protect your heart. If you see your FWB getting along with your family and friends at a barbecue, for example, you could develop feelings for him. (It's hard not to when your friends are cooing, "Oh, he's so cute! I really like him!")

Rule 5: You DON'T have to sleep over.
Jemma, a 25-year-old single woman in New Jersey, says one of her favorite parts of having a FWB is that she doesn't have to cuddle or have an awkward morning after. "I can

kick him out after the deed is done," she says. "For me, post-sex cuddling is all about emotional bonding and intimacy—and I have no interest in that with a sex buddy. I love saying goodnight, taking a hot shower and collapsing into bed totally relaxed...and satisfied."

Rule 6: DON'T get mad if your FWB goes out with someone else.
Remember, your FWB is not, we repeat, *not* your boyfriend. This means if you catch him with another girl on a date, he's not cheating on you. The same goes for him; you're free to date whomever you'd like.

Rule 7: DO keep your relationship in the bedroom.
After a few sexy nights spent with your FWB, you may start to wonder if you should meet for coffee, see a movie, or do some otherwise date-sequel activity. But Shaun, a single 24-year-old guy from Ohio, warns against it: "Unless you are planning to have a more serious relationship, a date leads someone to think that there's more to the sweaty tryst than just the physical aspect," he says.

Rule 8: DO protect yourself.
You should be practicing safe sex regardless of whom you're sleeping with, but it's crucial to be careful with a sex buddy because that's all he is—your buddy. And your pal could have multiple partners because he is not bound to you. "It is especially important to use condoms to prevent sexually transmitted infections [STIs] when engaging in casual sex, in addition to another reliable form of birth control to prevent pregnancy," says Lisa M. Valle, D.O., a board-certified obstetrician and gynecologist at Plaza-Towers Obstetrics and Gynecology in Santa Monica, Calif. She also recommends

131

getting tested for STIs every six months and, ideally, after each new partner.

Rule 9: DO be smart about social media.
Hey, maybe you met your FWB on Face book, but that doesn't mean he wants the world to know you're hooking up on the regular. Think twice before posting status updates like, "Bang in' time last night!" If you don't want to know what your FWB is up to in his spare time, you might also want to consider not connecting on Twitter and Face book to begin with.

Rule 10: DON'T think sex is required.
When Jazz, 31, who lives in California, started sleeping with her FWB, she says it was "freeing, adventurous, and so much fun that we did it multiple times a week and even met up on lunch breaks for romps in his car." After a few weeks, though, she got tired of doing it so often and declined one night. Once she explained that it had nothing to do with him and that she wasn't sleeping with someone else, the guy was fine with it. "From there on out, he never questioned me when I resisted, nor did I over think it when he ignored a text from me one late night," she says. "The thing about a sex buddy that is so cool is that if you play it for what it is, no one gets hurt. I suggest laying down the ground rules from day one."

Source http://www.glamour.com/sex-love-life/2012/10/10-rules-of-being-friends-with-benefits/

Chapter 14 – Hold on Bumpy ride!

Oh, Hell NO! Are you sleeping with the enemy?

Ladies, you might want to run on this one or carry around a microscope. Not only that, turn on the lights. You not only want the lights turned on, you might want to get a 1000 watt flash light.

Sexually transmitted diseases are no joke. None the less, these diseases are passed between women and men daily. So when he shows up at the door with flowers and a box of chocolates strawberries, maybe you need to be asking him *"what else do you have?"*

CELLPHONE SEXING!

I had a girlfriend who had men sexting her on her phone. At first I said that's really nasty and you should not be letting them send you body parts over the phone. Then she showed me the phone. Real talk… "I told her, you know this is not a bad idea because you can actually see the rolling pin without the cover and all its glory when you enlarge it."

She asked me would I have sex with him because he had such a big rolling pin. First, I said girl, I'm married! Then I said "Hell to the noooo…….." She said you're crazy because he has such a big rolling pin. I told her to enlarge that rolling pin again to see why I said "Hell to the noooo……"

133

It was like looking at that rolling pin through a fish bowl. He had more pimples and warts looking like a diamond mine on that rolling pin under the rim than rocky road ice cream. **Are you kidding me?**

If, you could put a rolling pin under a microscope to see if the man is carrying warts, just imagine how many times you would run the other way. By the way ladies you can catch genital warts from a man and it does not necessarily have to be on the rolling pin. They can be in the hair, on his back, under the twin sack etc…

This is one chapter under "sexually transmitted diseases" that women really need to keep close to the breast. Are you really checking out your partners or are you hooking up and jumping off.

Sisters, not all pregnancies are planned. The odds are greater when we do not education ourselves contraceptives. Woman have confessed that they have heard excuses from men not wanting to wear condoms. **Are you kidding me?** Don't buy in ladies.

After doing some research, these were the most hilarious excuses.

1. **"I will Pull out before I Shoot Out"**- Are men still using this line today? **Are you kidding me?**

2. **"It's The Woman's Responsibility to Handle Contraception"** Yes you're right, women need to protect themselves, however both parties are respon-

sible. Especially 9 months later if you know what I mean.

3. **"I Tear Open the Condom Package with My Teeth"- Do** you want children 9 months later? So you really believe those teeth will not put a hole in the condom.

4. **"Putting on or Taking off the Condom during Sex"** Are you kidding me? Why bother?

5. **"We Had Sex during Her Period" Are you really kidding me!** Now this is a good one! **Newsflash:** I agree, "Some women ovulate when they are menstruating, so next time while dipping into the Red Sea, be sure to use a life jacket".

6. **I've had the Condom for Three Years- Are you kidding me?** You really want to be pushing that stroller nine months later.

7. **I Like My Condom Tight', Are you kidding me?** Hello, hello, this will lead to the condom bursting.

8. **We Had S ex While Standing' Hmmm…   Are you kidding?**

Eight (8) Silly Things Men Do during Sex That Leads to Pregnancy – Titles were obtain from Source: http://www.omolove.com /2015/07/8-silly-things-men-do-during-se-x-that.html

In physics, following the law of gravity, it makes sense. But not in biology, which may have a law somewhere that states 'what goes in, stays in'. You should know that the "cookies" is one place that may not have a door but has a way of keeping things in. Be Warned! Basically, just don't be stupid during Sex. Protect yourself and your woman. Use a condom.

This is a huge one that you really need to educate yourself on, and continue to do research. You can also go to www.cdc.gov for a reference point of updated information. Women are always talking about how size matters. Before you think about going down south or letting him use every single hole in your body, this out.

All Below Are Sexually Transmitted Diseases;

Chlamydia: Chlamydia is actually a group of different infections caused by different strains of the Chlamydia bacterium: **1)** *Chlamydia pneumonia* causes a type of walking pneumonia **2)** *Chlamydia psittaci* causes a type of pneumonia caused by birds **3)** *Chlamydia trachomatis* causes various sexually transmitted diseases. **Chlamydia** (pronounced "Klamydia") is discussed along with gonorrhea because the symptoms that it causes are very similar to gonorrhea. In general, it tends to be a bit milder of a disease but this is not always so and it can cause many complications too. Like gonorrhea, Chlamydia is also very common with over a million new cases each year in the United States.

These germs can be found in the genitals, throat, and the anal canal of an infected person. They can also affect the eyes but this is uncommon. The groups most likely to get gonorrhea and Chlamydia are young adults from ages 15 to 29. There are more cases of gonorrhea and Chlamydia in the 15 to 19 year old age group when you consider that 15 to 19 year olds are less sexually active than 20 to 29 year olds.

The risk of spreading these diseases from a woman to a man following a single act of vaginal intercourse is said to be about 20 percent and it is likely that the rate of spread from men to women is even higher for each single act of sex. *A big problem is that ten to fifteen percent of men and about seventy five percent of women do not have any symptoms.* Most men and women who have symptoms will stop having sex and seek treatment. It is these individuals without symptoms who are spreading the disease more without even knowing it. When diagnosed, Chlamydia can be easily treated and cured. Untreated, Chlamydia can cause serious long and short term health problems in men and women as well as in newborn babies of infected mothers, including pelvic inflammatory disease (PID), which can cause: 1) Infertility 2) Tubal pregnancy (which can sometimes be fatal)

GONORRHEA: Gonorrhea Gonococcal Infection (clap, drip)

Gonorrhea is spread through sexual contact including: penis to vagina, including:
- Penis to vagina (infection rate for males 30-50%, females 60-90%)
- penis to mouth,
- penis to rectum

- mouth to vagina

Gonorrhea is: an infection that is spread through sexual contact with another person
- caused by a bacterium, *Neisseria gonorrhea*
- Second only to Chlamydia infections in the number of reported cases.

The Gonorrhea germs are found in the mucous areas of the body: Genital tract, Penis, Rectum, Throat, Vagina

Gonorrhea is: an infection that is spread through sexual contact with another person: caused by a bacterium, *Neisseria gonorrhea;* second only to Chlamydial infections in the number of reported cases.

The Gonorrhea germs are found in the mucous areas of the body: Genital tract, Penis, Rectum, Throat, Vagina

In women: The opening (cervix) to the womb (uterus) from the birth canal is the first place of infection ; The disease can spread into the womb and fallopian tubes, resulting in Pelvic Inflammatory Disease (PID) which can cause infertility in up to 10% of infected women and tubal (ectopic) pregnancy

Risk Groups: Any person who is sexually active can be infected with Gonorrhea
- Common among younger people, ages 15-30, who have multiple sex partners
- Increases in Gonorrhea have been found among men who have sex with men urban areas than in rural areas

- It is the most common reportable sexually transmitted infection in the United States, with an estimated 800,000 cases of Gonorrhea reported annually
- Occurs more frequently in urban areas than in rural areas

It is the most common reportable sexually transmitted infection in the United States, with an estimated 800,000 cases of Gonorrhea reported annually

GENITAL WARTS

- Caused by a virus (the Human Papilloma Virus or HPV)
- Appear as one or many raised lumps or bumps
- They appear 1 month to 1 year after having sex with an infected person.
- Often cannot be seen in women because they may be all inside the vagina. May also be too small in men and women to be easily seen.

More serious in women because they may change into cancer. About 30 types of Human Papilloma Virus are spread through sexual contact and can infect the genital area: *anus, cervix, penis, rectum, scrotum, vagina, and vulva*

Human Papilloma Virus (HPV) is a viral infection of the skin and is sometimes also called, *anogenital warts, condylomata acuminate, genital warts, venereal warts*. It causes growths of skin-colored, cauliflower-like masses of various sizes and shapes. It is thought there are more cases of genital Human Papilloma Virus (HPV) infection than any other STD in the United States, infecting from 3-28% of the population, with up to 5 million new cases reported every year.

Human Papilloma Virus (HPV) lives in skin cells and may be confined to an early isolated outbreak or may be located internally in the: rectum, throat, urethra, and vagina **Symptoms** may occur several weeks to months after being exposed to Human Papilloma Virus (HPV) and include: **1)** Itching or burning around the sex organs **2)** Painless growths in either sex usually on damp or moist surfaces of the body beginning as tiny, soft pink or red spots **3)** Spots develop into small, white/yellow/gray bumpy warts on the sex organs and anus **4)** Warts can grow quickly into irregularly shaped cauliflower-like masses.

HEPATITIS: Hepatitis is a disease which causes inflammation of the liver, and sometimes death. There are 4 forms of hepatitis (A, B, C and D), only the sexually transmitted ones (Hepatitis A and B) will be discussed here. **Hepatitis A** is caused by the Hepatitis A Virus and is highly contagious. It is transmitted by: fecal-oral contact
Hepatitis B is caused by the Hepatitis B Virus [HBV]. It is found in:

- blood
- fecal matter
- saliva
- urine

There are up to 200,000 infections reported per year and up to 33% of Americans have evidence of some past infection (immunity).

HERPES SIMPLEX VIRUS: Herpes is a sexually transmitted disease (STD) caused by a virus known as the Herpes Simplex Virus (HSV). Genital herpes infection is very common and on the increase in the United States. It is more common in women (1 out of 4) than in men (1 out of 5) possibly because male to female transmission is more efficient than female to male transmission.

- Caused by a virus germ.
- Appears 3 to 10 days after sex with person who already has the disease.
- The herpes sores start as blisters, then they open up into little holes, and then they scab up.
- By 5 to 15 days they heal and disappear.
- The germs stay in your body and the sores may return in the future, sometimes often.
- Women may not know they have herpes because the sores may be inside the vagina.

Herpes is spread by direct skin contact including: <u>Sexual contact:</u>   Anal sex, Oral sex, vaginal sex, as well as, Kissing, Skin-to-skin contact which transmits HSV-1 and HSV-2. **<u>Genital herpes: 1)</u> Can be transmitted with or without the presence of sores or other symptoms 2)** Is often transmitted by people who do not realize infection can be passed on even when there are no symptoms **3)** Is often transmitted by people unaware they are infected

Statistics: 1) An estimated 40 million people in the US have genital herpes which is a chronic viral infection **2)** About 500,000 new people get diagnosed with herpes each year in the US **3)** There are even more people without symptoms

PELVIC INFLAMMATORY DISEASE (PID): when caused by the <u>Chlamydia bacteria</u> may result in only minor symptoms, sometimes with no symptoms at all, even though it can seriously damage the reproductive organs **Gonorrhea Bacteria:** Symptoms of Pelvic Inflammatory Disease (PID) caused by the <u>Gonorrhea Bacteria</u> often begin immediately after menstruation rather than at any other time during the menstrual cycle, although this has not been proven in Chlamydia Pelvic Inflammatory Disease (PID)

Pelvic Inflammatory Disease (PID) is a progressive infection and inflammation, which can result in substantial damage to a woman's reproductive system. Many different organisms can cause Pelvic Inflammatory Disease, but most cases are usually caused by the bacteria:

- *Neisseria gonorrhoeae*
- *Chlamydia trachomatis*

Pelvic inflammatory disease (PID) usually occurs in sexually active women between the ages of 15-25 and the highest rate of infection is among teenagers and adolescents. More than 750,000 new cases of Pelvic Inflammatory Disease (PID) are diagnosed every year in the U.S. The cervix usually prevents bacteria in the vagina from spreading up into the internal organs but if the cervix is exposed to a

142

sexually transmitted disease (STD), such as Gonorrhea or Chlamydia, the cervix becomes infected. The gonococcus, *Neisseria gonorrhea: 1)* moves upwards to the fallopian tubes, where it casts out some cells and invades other cells 2) multiplies within and beneath these cells 3) spreads to other organs resulting in more inflammation and scarring

SYPHILLI: is a sexually transmitted disease (STD) caused by a bacterium (*Treponema palladium*). The initial infection causes an ulcer at the site of infection. **Syphilis**, once virtually untreatable, can nowadays be effectively diagnosed and treated with antibiotic therapy. **Early symptoms** of syphilis are often very mild, and treatment is often not sought when first infected. Syphilis increases the risk of transmitting and receiving the human immunodeficiency virus (HIV). Over time, the bacteria moves throughout the body, causes damage too many organs. **The disease is divided into four stages: 1)** Primary 2) Secondary 3) Latent 4) Tertiary (late). An untreated infected person may infect others during the first 2 stages (1-2 years). In an infected person the bacterium spreads from the initial ulcer to the skin or mucous membranes of: **1)** the anus of a sexual partner **2)** the genital area **3)** the mouth. The bacterium can pass through broken skin on parts of the body.

The syphilis bacterium is very fragile and infection is usually spread by

- an infected pregnant woman who can pass the bacterium to her unborn baby, which can result in the child being born with serious mental and physical problems
- sexual contact

TRICHOMONIASIS: is a common sexually transmitted disease caused by a single-cell parasitic protozoan, *Trichomonas vaginitis,* which was first discovered in 1836. About 5 million Americans develop trichomoniasis every year. It has been found in: 1) 5%-15% of women at gynecology clinics 2) 50%-75% of prostitutes in the United States   It is often diagnosed in patients who are already infected with other STDs such as: 1) gonorrhea 2) nongonococcal urethritis (NGU). The parasite rarely causes symptoms in men and re-infection of women by untreated partners can often occur. **It can be spread during:** anal sex; mutual masturbation when bodily fluids from one partner come in contact with the other's genitals (in rare cases); oral sex; vaginal sex. Unlike most STDs, Trichomonas can survive for some hours outside the body on infected objects and can be transmitted by sharing:

- bodily fluids
- contaminated bedding
- damp towels
- sheets
- toilet seats

Chancroid (Kan-kroid) is also known as: 1) soft chancre 2) venereal sore Infection from Chancroid related to *Haemophilus ducreyi* is decreasing in many areas but increasing in infections related to Herpes simplex virus type-2 (HSV-2). Chancroid is a bacterial disease causing painful, irregularly shaped sores, but is a localized infection which can be treated and cured and has no long-term effects. Over 4,000 cases are reported annually occurring

HIV stands for Human Immunodeficiency Virus; the virus causes AIDS, and is an infection of the immune system which destroys the body's ability to fight off infections. HIV may also enter a cell then remain quiet for a long time and drug therapy only destroys the active virus. HIV infects the cells (T Lymphocytes) of the immune system weakening the entire system.

AIDS: stands for: **Acquired** which means: you were not born with the disease compared to most immune deficient conditions

*You can only be born with AIDS if your mother had AIDS when pregnant. **Immunodeficiency** which means: the disease is characterized by a weakened or ineffective immune system with no resistance to infections -**Syndrome** which means: AIDS is a combination of signs and symptoms.

SOURCE: 1) www.medicinenet.com; 2) www.herpes-coldsores.com; 3) www.healthac.org; 4) www.mshc.otg.au;5) www.medscape.com; 6) www.cdc.gov; http://www.cdc.gov/std/default.htm;

Internet's Dirty Secret: Assessing the Impact of Online Intermediaries on the Outbreak of Sexually Transmitted Diseases

Jason Chan New York University - Leonard N. Stern School of Business & Anindya Ghose New York University - Leonard N. Stern School of Business
April 6, 2012
Abstract: *We investigate how the expansion of Craigslist into different states over a 11 year period in the United States affected the incidence of HIV. Using a natural experiment setup, we identify the effects of Craigslist's entry on HIV trends by exploiting the variations across states and time. After controlling for extraneous factors, our results show that Craigslist's entry leads to a 19.8 percent increase in HIV cases, which maps out to an average of 158.7 cases for a state in a year. The analyses further suggest that non-market related casual sex serves as the underlying mechanism driving the increase in HIV cases, while paid transactions (e.g., escort services and prostitution) solicited on the site do not influence HIV trends. The increases in HIV cases as a result of Craigslist entry are estimated to impose treatment costs of over $118 million annually on the U.S. healthcare system. Study implications and limitations are discussed.*

SOURCE: File Name: SSRN-id2150282.; © 2013 Social Science Electronic Publishing

Chapter 15 – Are we being Needy & Greedy?

Sister to Sister, can we get down with it and talk? Can we discuss the following twenty-seven issues? Are we being Needy and Greedy?

"Sex is not all making 'love' and orgasms is it"?

As women who are the evolution in GOD plan, we need to learn how to satisfy our own innermost needs and stop looking to men to satisfy those needs. Your happiness should not be men dependent. Learn what makes you happy and then you can join with a man to make a loving happy relationship.

Are we not listing to our men? Can you identify with any of the 27 thing below? Some of the words have been changed to keep a "G" rating.

Hilarious!!!!!!!!!!!!!!!!!!!!

27 things women do during sex that men hate by Hannah Gale for Metro.co.uk

1. 'Biting, in a bad way. When giving *"service"* *(word change)*, please keep your teeth away from my rolling pin. It is not a meal.'

2. 'When you change into hideous "comfy" pajamas as soon as the sex is over, especially if they resemble your late grandmother's curtains.'

3. 'If, as soon as you take off your *"undies"(word change)*, the room smells like a fish market – at that point it is my legal right to wind things up.'

4. 'Banning me from sex if you come up with the idea to spice things up by watching porn together, then you get pissed off because I get a *"stainless steel rolling pin (change words)"*-on from watching it.'

5. 'When you watch TV over our shoulder. Not cool.'

6. 'Two words: Vice grip. The objective isn't to pull the d….n thing off.'

7. 'Whatever your friends tell you or what you may read on the internet, you should ask before you try to slip a finger up a man's *"backdoor" (change word)* We may not appreciate it.'

8. 'Being slapped in the face during sex. Do not try to break my jaw. It hurts. A lot.'

9. 'When you stop making an effort with your *"undies" (change word)*. I don't want to see your granny pants on a daily basis.'

10. 'If you're a squinter, please warn us first. It can be quite the surprise and spare bed clothes should be prepared.'

11. 'When you're not respectful of flat mates when I bring you back home. Nothing's more embarrassing than a girl screaming like she's being murdered then having to face everyone afterwards.'

12. 'Cuddling. We get it, it's nice, but sometimes you just take it too far.'

13. 'Riling me up with the filthiest of dirty talk beforehand, only to then lay there like a corpse. Talk is cheap.'

14. 'Going way over the top with noises – I once received a noise complaint, it's thoroughly embarrassing.'

15. 'When you do a dead starfish. Please don't just lie there and do nothing, it's the least sexy thing ever.'
16. 'When we want to have sex and you say you're too tired. That makes us very sad.'
17. 'When you fall asleep halfway through. Mortifying.'
18. 'When you give us a *"service" (change word)* and then run off to spit everything out the moment we've finished. Come on, be a bit more discreet.'
19. 'Sometimes after we've had sex we just want to go to sleep. Please don't get annoyed when we don't want to stay up and talk.'
20. 'When you ask 100 questions, especially after sex. Please don't ask, "How was that for you?" Not ever.'
23. 'When you take it really personally when we can't orgasm. Especially when you say, "Was it something I did?"'
24. 'Bringing up your ex before/during/after. Just no.'
25. 'When you start running/waddling out of the room immediately after to "clean up".'
26. 'When you go into your friend's room straight afterwards to have a good gossip about the encounter while I am still in the house. Err…'
27. 'When you go to the loo with the door open before or after sex – or worse, just as things are about to get going. So gross.'

SOURCE: http://metro.co.uk/2014/10/22/27-things-women-do-during-sex-that-men-hate-4719543/#ixzz3iEjMq5xj

GUYS, the rest of this chapter is for you!
Some men seem to always be attracted to the following women character traits. Why?

Abusive Man "bully"

Seven Types of Women Men Should Avoid Dating in 2011

Married and taken- Guys if the woman you come across has a boyfriend or husband leave her alone because sometimes these women are ill-equipped to communicate with the men in their lives when problems arise, and it doesn't do you any good to be involved with that kind of woman. It's not only disrespectful, but you wouldn't want some other man coming on or making passes at your wife or girlfriend. If you're being approached by that kind of woman send her home. She's not worth your time she has nothing to offer you anyway.

Hood rats and felons-This is a growing problem with men today they will disregard women who are intelligent, classy, educated and have their stuff together for a loud, ignorant, obnoxious and classless woman who comes off as someone who has no home training. Why would you want a woman like this in your life? If you had a good woman dating or married why would you give that up for something that needs to stay in the trash? Hood rats are only going to bring you problems down the line and they're not the kind of women you need to be bringing your family and friends. Step your game up by leaving the trash where it belongs and keep your game on point by dismissing women who don't

come correct with what is expected of a potential mate.

High maintenance and Overly-flirty Divas-This type of woman can be the most aggravating to deal with because she's constantly surrounded by men and if she doesn't have a balance in her friends meaning she's got equal number of male and female friends. You want someone who's not constantly craving attention from the male audience. A woman usually doesn't have that many male friends and if she's got more male than female friends that's a red flag and a sign that she's an excessive flirt. Don't waste your time with a woman like this she's one that doesn't really change. Women who are too high maintenance are often insecure and stuck on themselves and these women need to be left where you found them. Deal with women who are level headed and down to earth they make better conversation than someone who cares more about her image than a stable relationship.

Emotionally and psychologically weak-Women who don't have it in them to handle their own are ones you don't want to deal with. One example such is women who allow other men to interfere and come between them and their boyfriends. A woman who is confident and strong will be able to handle a man that is secure. If she can't think and feel for her, and needs someone else to relay messages to someone to decipher her feelings or allows someone else to taunt her boyfriend or husband especially if she cheated clearly shows a lack of maturity and childish behavior.

Financially irresponsible-This is another one to watch out for because you don't want to deal with someone who can't pay their bills on time or spends her money wisely. This is not the kind of woman you need to really be dealing with because she'll expect you to pay for things she can take care of herself. If she can't pay a bill on time or manage to keep a significant amount of money in the bank and not constantly drawing out money to use and not budgeting her money sensibly for everyday things outside of bills. She's buying things she does not need or on impulse which is a sign of financial irresponsibility and constantly overdrawing her bank account(s) and maxing out credit cards. A woman who is financially responsible would be pretty diligent about what she spends her money on and keeps her bills paid on time and her responsibilities in check. Huge red flag is a woman with bad credit and lawsuits because she owes people money you don't want to deal with someone like that because that's a huge giveaway of someone who's financially irresponsible.

Lacking employment and educational standards-Chronic unemployment is a sign of immaturity because a woman who is mature will have some kind of gainful employment and some educational standards. If she hasn't made advancements in her educational life such as seeking a degree or finishing up school like getting her GED or something saying she went to school that's a sign that she hasn't grown up yet. A woman who is mature will have a plan in place for her future and has a definite and concrete timeline of completing her studies or when she graduates from a college or trade school program. A mature woman also will be in the market actively looking for a job and isn't on some BS as to why she isn't looking for a job.

Living at home with parent(s)-It's one thing to live at home if you're caring for your elderly or sick parent(s), but when you're past the age of 25 and you're still living at home with your parent(s) with no real incentive to move out and get your own place it is a clear sign she's being enabled by her mother or father and that she's not mature enough to get out on her own. If you come across women who are still shacked up at home, and they're pushing thirty or in their thirties or older to drop them like a bad habit because it's these same women who seek out the established and stable men who have their program in order. Don't bother with women who are still living at home with their parent(s) because they're being enabled to grow up and assume adult level responsibilities.

In meeting women always check out her character and personality. If you meet a good woman who's got her head on straight and is down to earth don't let her go because good women don't come along often. As a man you should want someone who will make a good partner or spouse for you. Someone you would bring around your family and friends.

Keep in mind if your family and friends are hinting to you that the woman you are dating is not someone suited for you pay close attention. You would be surprised how the people around you can see things in the person you're dating that you can't see. Part of dating is to not settle for less. If you had a good woman who you traded in for someone who is not up to standards it's time to re-evaluate you're dating standards as to why you would take up with someone who is a loser.

As a man you set your own standards in dating as to the kind of women you attract and if you attract trash and scum there's something about you that brings those types of women to your life. If you have a good woman who treats you good and respects you that's a blessing, but if you have someone convincing you that the good woman you're with is "mistreating" you badly you're allowing someone to tell you otherwise not letting you determine if the person you're with is treating you well. Don't settle for someone who is not up to standards and if you got someone who is good to you don't let them go. If someone is interfering with your relationship be a man and let that woman know you are in a relationship and would appreciate it if she didn't interfere and to back off. Unsuitable women are ones you should never give a minute of your time. If you find a good woman appreciate her and don't let her go.

*C*hapter **16 –A** House Built with Love!

Do you simply want the wedding or the true essence of a loving relationship?

When women get engaged, it's supposed to be the happiest time in their entire lives apart from giving birth to their children. We put some much energy into planning a wedding for that one "day" and it must be PERFECT! We want that perfect ring, perfect venue, perfect cake, perfect dress and of course the perfect braid maids. Yes, everything must be perfect that "DAY"!

Image, if we could simply harvest some of the perfection and energy that we put into that one day into your marriage, it would be perfectly everlasting.

I'm sure you hear every day how peoples spend millions to billions of dollars on the perfect wedding, only to be married a nanosecond. So I ask you Sister to Sister of all ethnic background, do you want the perfect "Day" or the "Life Time".

After 30 years of marriage to my husband, I might know a few little things that can be shared with my Sister girls! I want to leave you with a listed below which are 10 good habits that should be applied to keeping a relationship strong by: Good Faith printed on MSN Dec 19, 2013.

The 10 habits that keep marriages strong

1) Not trying to change each other: The key to wedded bliss isn't over-the-top romance, but these surprisingly simple practices you can do to stay - or fall back - in love with your partner. Read on for expert tips on how to have a happy marriage. Maybe you wish he folded his socks, or that he would chat it up with your friends without prompting. But, his inability to notice hair in the sink may stem from the laid-back personality that drew you to him in the first place. "One of the things we see with happy couples is that they know their partner's differences, and have pretty much stopped trying to change the other person," says Darren Wilk, a certified Gottman Couples Therapist with a private practice in Vancouver, British Columbia. "Rather than trying to fight their partner's personality style, they instead focus on each other's strengths."

2) Framing your demands as favors: Whether you want him to unload the dishwasher more often or pay closer attention to the kids, your partner will be more likely to change his behavior if he feels like he'll get relationship brownie points. "Throw it out there like a favor. Present it like 'here is the recipe for what will make me happy,' because everyone wants to make their partner feel happy," says Wilk. "When you present your needs, present them as what you do want rather than what you don't want." Instead of saying, "I hate when you have to have everything sched-

uled," try saying, "I would love to have a day where we can just be spontaneous."

3) Vocalizing your appreciation: Giving your partner positive reinforcement sounds like a no-brainer, but couples often forget to do it. "Relationship expert Gottman's research found that in everyday life, happy couples have 20 positive moments, such as a shared look, compliment, or affectionate touch, to every negative moment," says Wilk. Tell him something positive three times a day, and be specific. Instead of saying, "You're a good dad," tell him why. "You're a good dad because you helped our daughter with that puzzle, which I never would have had the patience to do."

4) Focusing on the positive: "Unhappy couples are stuck in a negative state of mind," says Wilk. "You will always find what you look for. If you look for stuff that bugs you and that your partner is doing wrong, you will find it every day. If you look at what your partner is doing it right, you'll find it every day." It's a choice to flip your mindset, so when you find yourself getting annoyed, visualize something he does that makes your heart flutter to halt the negative thought circuit

5) Taking trips down memory lane: "Happy couples tend to rewrite history by glossing over the bad stuff and focusing on the happy times," says Wilk. By reliving memories out loud to your partner, it actually changes your mindset, and how you view him and think about your relationship. Try this exercise whenever you feel your relationship needs a boost: Go over the highlights of when you were first dating, or rehearse the best moments of your relationship (such as the day you had an impromptu picnic in the park during your lunch hour, or that surprise anniversary date he took you on) to uncover buried memories.

6) Never siding with the enemy: "Sometimes what affair-proofs a relationship is simply being there when your partner needs to vent, and having their back without try-

ing to fix the problem," says Wilk. "People want someone to listen to them. The key is to be supportive, and never take the side of the person he's venting about, even if you can see where that person is coming from. For example, if he is upset that his boss took away a contract and gave it to someone else in the office, now is not the time to say, "Well, maybe you didn't put your best effort in." Right now he needs his feelings validated, and to hear you say, "That must have been really hard." Happy couples know when to bite their tongues.

7) Not getting too comfortable: Trust, security, and commitment are key elements in any relationship, but having them doesn't mean you can treat your relationship as rock-solid, and stop trying. "Relationships are a fragile ecosystem, and that's why there is a 50 percent divorce rate," says Wilk. "Happy couples keep dating, telling each other they look great, and doing things together."

8) Having rituals of connection: "It's not only about having a date night, but happy couples seem to do a lot of mundane things together," says Wilk. "They have little habits that they decide to do together, whether it is sitting down to pay the bills once a month or folding laundry." We say anything to make that pile of dirty clothes feel more manageable.

9) Knowing your partner's calls for attention: Happy couples are mindful of those little moves their partners do for attention. When Gottman's team studied 120 newlyweds in his Love Lab, they discovered that couples who stayed married six years later were paying attention to these bids for connection 86 percent of the time, compared to only 33 percent of the time for those who later divorced. So, look out for the little things, and respond to his need to connect. Like if you're grocery shopping and he casually mentions that he hasn't had Fruit Loops since he was a kid, throw them in the cart for him to show that you care.

10) Doing the little things: "When it comes to relationship satisfaction, you can't just ride on the big things like, 'I don't drink, I pay the bills, I don't beat you, we went to Hawaii last year,'" says Wilk. "This stuff is not really what keeps couples happy in their daily lives." What really matters is all the small stuff that adds up, such as being there for each other when one needs to vent, or noticing when he needs a hug, or making him his favorite meal just because. "It's also giving up on the idea that you have to feel in love all the time. Marriage is about trust

About The Author

Adrian Tisdale is an entrepreneur, Author, Radio Host, Teacher, Trainer, Counselor, Inspirational Speaker, Wife, Mother, and Grandmother. She is a native of Brooklyn New York. Adrian was the founder and Executive Director for Alternative Inc. in the Commonwealth of Virginia, a HIV/AIDS organization which provided counseling and case management to HIV positive adults and children. She was a Certified Advance Resource Technology, Inc. National Regional Train the Trainer for the Federal Government. Adrian certified trained in Substance Abuse, and HIV/AID. Under the Northern Virginia Planning District, she served for the committee to develop the Ryan White Care Bill Act.

Ms. Tisdale has been interviewed on the Nationally Syndicated Clark Howard of the Clark Howard Show, Atlanta, and Jim Strickland, WSBTV, Channel 2 News Investigator, to heighten consumer's awareness. Her love and ability to help others led her to write "Are You Kidding Me" as a tool to help adults globally. She wants to establish a connection and help promote loving relationships and emotional awareness in adults. She is a frequent and available keynote speaker.

Adrian M. Tisdale, LLC
Wall Street Executive Suites
2385 Wall Street, Suite 340
Conyers Georgia 30013

Phone: (678) 964-4934
Phone: (678) 964-2320 ext. 340
Fax: (678) 203-2118

Email info@adriantisdale.com
Web: www.adriantisdale.com

Please follow us on:

Facebook: Adrian M Tisdale
LinkedIn: Adrian M Tisdale
Twitter: Adrian M Tisdale
Instagram: #areyoukiddingme
                #adriantisdale

Look for the second book in the **Are You Kidding Me Series**
Copyright © 2015 coming fall of 2016.